MW00812302

ASSET MANAGEMENT FOR ENDOWMENTS AND FOUNDATIONS

ASSET MANAGEMENT FOR ENDOWMENTS AND FOUNDATIONS

Improving Investment Performance and Reducing Management Costs

WILLIAM SCHNEIDER

ROBERT DIMEO

D. ROBINSON CLUCK

McGraw-Hill

New York   San Francisco   Washington, D.C.   Auckland   Bogotá
Caracas   Lisbon   London   Madrid   Mexico City   Milan
Montreal   New Delhi   San Juan   Singapore
Sydney   Tokyo   Toronto

Library of Congress Cataloging-in-Publication Data

Schneider, William, date.
    Asset management for endowments and foundations : improving
investment performance & reducing management costs / William
Schneider, Robert DiMeo, D. Robinson Cluck.
      p. cm.
    ISBN 0–7863–1070–7
     1. Endowments—United States—Finance. 2. Foundations—United
States—Finance. 3. Investment banking—United States. 4. Asset
allocation—United States. I. DiMeo, Robert A. II. Cluck, D.
Robinson.   III. Title.
HV95.S36 1997
361.7'63'0681—dc21

                                          97–9620
                                            CIP

McGraw-Hill

A Division of The *McGraw-Hill* Companies

  2 3 4 5 6 7 8 9 0 DOC/DOC 9 0 2 1 0 9 8 7

ISBN 0–7863–1070–7

The sponsoring editor for this book was *Steven Sheehan,* the editing supervisor was
Donna Namorato, and the production supervisor was *Suzanne W. B. Rapcavage.* It
was set in Palatino by *Bruce Hendrickson.*

Printed and bound by R. R. Donnelley & Sons Company.

This publication is designed to provide accurate and authoritative information
in regard to the subject matter covered. It is sold with the understanding that
neither the author or the publisher is engaged in rendering legal, accounting,
or other professional service. If legal advice or other expert assistance is required,
the services of a competent professional person should be sought.

    —*From a Declaration of Principles jointly adopted by a Committee*
     of the American Bar Association and a Committee of Publishers.

CONTENTS

Chapter 13

Hiring a Consultant   201

Chapter 14

Reduce Costs   215

Chapter 15

Conclusion   223

Index   229

PREFACE

"This is going to be harder than I imagined," Smitty thought as the others continued their heated debate.

"I think that the best way to make money is NOT to lose money," MacDougal commented, irritation showing in his voice.

Cal Jordan scowled slightly but stood his ground. "My wife always says that you just need to ride out bad markets. We can't continue our spending policy if we only earn CD rates." His wife was Managing Partner of Saunders Weiss & Jordan. She and Cal had personally contributed over $100,000 to the foundation.

Jason Bender, the foundation's president, said soothingly, "I think that Mr. MacDougal is trying to remind us of what happened in 1994. You weren't on the investment committee then, Mr. Jordan, but we put half the funds with a money manager who came with the highest of recommendations. Well, it was an absolute disaster. We kept our spending policy at 8% and the assets actually lost 4%. At that time . . ."

MacDougal interrupted, "We pulled the plug before we got further behind; we wouldn't even have had a foundation left at that rate."

"To give the Devil his due, if we'd just left the money with the manager, we'd have made it all back and more in '95," added Larry Ballinger in a deferential tone. Larry was the foundation's treasurer; he had been a partner with one of the Big Eight accounting firms before consolidation turned it into the Big Six.

"I didn't build my company by rolling the dice," snapped MacDougal, "and I don't think that we should gamble with the foundation's funds either." His face was two shades redder than normal. He was a man who was not used to being challenged.

Smitty took advantage of the silence that followed to begin in a quiet tone. "I know I'm a brand-new member of the finance

committee, but I do sit on the board of my company's pension plan
and I can tell you that over the past 10 years we've earned in
excess of 12 percent per year. Our investment policy has a target
allocation of 60 percent stocks and 40 percent bonds. We've got
some of the equity portion in foreign stocks and some in small
company stocks . . ."

"I'd be opposed to foreign stocks," blurted out Cal, surprised
to find himself on the same side of the fence as MacDougal.

"That was my reaction at first," continued Smitty, "but our
consultant showed how we could actually reduce risk by . . ."

"We've never used a consultant," interrupted Jason. "We
have some financial horsepower right here on our board." He
smiled toward John Sparrow.

John was a managing director with one of the largest brokerage firms in the country. He had risen through the ranks from
bond salesman to sales manager to branch manager to his current
position as regional manager. Responding to Jason's cue, he
began, "Our investment strategist is cautious on the market right
now. Usually the year following a presidential election is the
weakest in the political cycle." He prided himself on never missing the morning research call. "Although," he added "long term,
we like equities."

At that moment Roland Keller cleared his throat slightly, as if
to signal that he was ready to make a pronouncement. Roland was,
far and away, the largest donor to the foundation. His generosity
had already extended well into six figures, and his opinion counted
for a lot. "Perhaps we were overly hasty in abandoning the stock
market. It probably wouldn't hurt to have a little more exposure."

"But," he added, raising his forefinger for emphasis, "the
key to maintaining our spending policy is more active fundraising. We need to dig a little deeper and to encourage our friends to
do so as well."

If you are on the board of a foundation or endowment, the above dialogue may sound familiar. Such boards are usually filled with bright, successful, high-powered people who have volunteered their time and usually some of their money. The finance committee is often large, with varying levels of financial sophistication on the part of the members. There is often a fair amount of turnover among the committee members. The dynamics of such a group can be challenging. Add to this a 5 percent spending requirement and stock and bond markets which have become increasingly global as well as more volatile. It's not surprising that most foundations and endowments have a tough time developing and implementing sound investment policy.

The goal of this book is to help you create a framework to integrate your organization's goals, spending policy, and investment strategy. We will also help you make some decisions about asset allocation. We'll give you an approach to develop an appropriate investment policy. You will be shown some of the latest techniques in manager selection. You'll see how to set up a systematic and effective way to evaluate the performance of your investments, and last but not least, you will learn methods to reduce your expenses.

Who should read this book? Any foundation or endowment donor or board member; advisors, including accountants, consultants, and attorneys; and other service providers such as bankers, brokers, and money managers. In short, this book is for anyone who has an interest in controlling the risk, enhancing the return, and reducing the cost of managing endowment and foundation assets.

ACKNOWLEDGMENTS

First and foremost, we'd like to thank Matthew R. McArthur of M. R. McArthur & Associates, Ltd., Hinsdale, Illinois. Matt wrote the bulk of Chapter 12, "Fiduciary Issues."

We would also like to gratefully acknowledge Steven Hardy and Zephyr Associates for providing the software as well as advice and counsel which were essential to Chapter 8, "Style." In addition, Christina Sbarra, Senior Data Analyst, Canterbury Consulting, provided substantial assistance in the development of Chapters 3, 4, and 11.

Additionally, we'd like to thank the following professionals of DiMeo Schneider & Associates, L.L.C.: Barry Livingston, Consultant, who wrote a portion of Chapter 12 and performed a great deal of the research; Laura Schneider, Director of Administration, who provided invaluable assistance in producing and assembling this manuscript; Trina Solomon, Senior Analyst, who produced most of the graphic exhibits and sample performance reports; Linda Coffey, Vice President, and Greg Johnsen, Vice President, for their contributions to the manager search and goal setting chapters; and also Mike Benoit, Debbie Weix, Stephanie Tatum, and Jackie Gray for their support.

Lastly, we'd like to thank our wives, Caren Schneider, Adriane DiMeo, and Tammi Cluck, for all their encouragement.

1

CHAPTER

Asset Management for Endowments and Foundations

OVERVIEW

If you serve on the board of a foundation or endowment, you are among the best and the brightest in American society. Typically board members volunteer their time, effort, and in many cases their money to advance a cause in which they believe. They are intelligent people, often highly successful in their own field. Our belief is that smart people make good decisions . . . if they are given good information. Hopefully this book will give you the information you need.

Foundations and endowments exist to serve various noble goals. Some seek to further higher education; others to fight disease, hunger, or hundreds of other ills which plague society. Some exist to exalt the human spirit, offering grants to foster dance, music, or the visual arts. Still others try to further our understanding of ourselves. Religion, philosophy, and psychology have all benefited from grants.

Behind these higher callings lies a very prosaic reality: Endowments and foundations exist to provide money. *Spending policy* is their reason to be. In fact, at least 5 percent of assets must be disbursed every year in order to preserve the tax-exempt status of the fund. Furthermore, most funds seek to provide money not just for today but into perpetuity. The collision of spending policy with the long-term realities of the capital markets can cause problems. Few assets provide a real return greater than 5 percent after inflation.

THE TICKING TIME BOMB

If spending policy is not linked to investment policy, then ultimately spending policy is in jeopardy. A common mistake is to target only *income* (i.e., dividends and interest). The problem is that income alone generally can't beat inflation. For example, consider an endowment which funds several scholarships as well as providing a chair at the local university.

During the 1980s a portfolio consisting primarily of bonds easily produced enough income to not only match the spending requirements of the endowment, but also to increase the fund from $11 million to over $20 million. However, now the board faces a challenge. Interest rates peaked in 1981 and then began a downward trend which continued until the beginning of 1994. Meanwhile, tuition costs continue to escalate at over 5 percent per year. The portfolio's current yield has dropped to a little over 6 percent. If something is not done the scholarships will provide a smaller and smaller percentage of the students' tuition. In real terms, the endowment has gone into liquidation.

Unfortunately, board members may not be able to place this problem in context, having been lulled into a false sense of security by the unusually strong returns of the last decade. Intermediate-term Government bonds produced a compound return of 11.91 percent per year from 1980 to 1989 versus an annual inflation rate of 5.09 percent for the decade.[1] Life was good! The problem is that the 1990s and beyond may be more like decades other than the '80s.

In the '40s bonds produced an inflation-adjusted return of minus 3.58 percent per year. In the '50s those same bonds produced **negative** 0.86 percent per year after inflation; in the '60s the number was positive . . . an anemic +0.96 percent per year. The '70s, of course, saw negative returns again.[2] So what's the solution? In the forthcoming chapters we'll discuss many strategies; however, all of them are based on the *total return* concept.

Even funds that targeted a rate of total return rather than income may be in trouble. In the '80s, returns for stocks were even more generous than for bonds. Human nature being what it is, many funds grew "fat and happy." There has been no great incentive to adopt cutting-edge techniques of financial oversight. In fact, many endowments and foundations have even allowed spending policy to expand beyond 5 percent. Good markets have masked flawed investment and spending policy.

THE NATURE OF BOARDS

As we said earlier, board members of eleemosynary institutions are generally bright, successful, committed people. They are usually honored to have been invited to their position and take their responsibilities very seriously. There is, however, a great incentive to avoid the embarrassment of advocating a strategy which causes the fund to lose money in a nominal sense. An unintended consequence of this situation may be that money is invested in a way that produces

---

1. Ibbotson Associates, *1996 SBBI Yearbook*, pp. 198–199.
2. Ibid.

too little return. We'll discuss that particular danger in the chapters on asset allocation.

A different type of problem may affect some boards. Often, strong, successful people have deeply ingrained opinions about the markets. Our experience is that some of those opinions are accurate and some are not. One persistent misconception is that stocks and bonds produce almost the same returns. The reality is that since 1926 large company stocks have enjoyed a compound return of 10.5 percent per year while intermediate U.S. Government bonds have produced only 5.3 percent per year. To translate that into more meaningful terms, $1,000,000 invested in intermediate U.S. Government bonds in 1926 grew to be $35,282,360 by the end of 1995. The same $1,000,000 invested in large S&P 500 type stocks grew to be *$1.1 billion!*[3] That same $1,000,000 invested in small company stocks grew to *$3.8 billion!*[4] One goal of this book is to give you an overview of investment fact and theory as a starting point for a well-reasoned investment program.

FUNDING AND FUNDRAISING

As if the capital markets didn't provide enough challenge, the current economic environment may prove even more difficult. In an era when politicians of both parties are arguing about cutbacks rather than how to increase spending, the outlook for government support of charitable activities is not rosy. A greater share of the burden will be placed on foundations and endowments. Institutions that once supplemented government spending may now find themselves to be the sole source. Furthermore, with companies facing increased global competition there may be less corporate

3. Ibid.
4. Ibid.

money available. Besides, corporate giving can be very difficult to explain to the survivors of a recent downsizing.

Individual donations may also drop in a more normal capital market environment. The inflation of the '70s combined with an onerous tax code to provide a great incentive to gift appreciated assets. The bull market of the '80s did the same. However, if returns are in the 7 to 10 percent range for the next few years there will be fewer dollars available. Even those who have the money to give may feel less wealthy and therefore be less generous. In short, fundraising is likely to become more difficult.

If a foundation or endowment is in a fundraising mode (and who isn't?) there may be motivation to be overly conservative. One can imagine an angry donor asking "You did *what* with the money?" Losses in the investment portfolio can make it difficult to "go back to the well." On the other hand, if you can demonstrate that you have a solid, well-conceived investment program you might find it easier to raise money. This book should help.

The next chapter outlines a proven approach to the oversight of foundation and endowment assets. The rest of the book will develop those concepts.

2

The Prudent Steward

Fortunately, there is a solution to the problems mentioned in the overview. Since the '50s, a body of financial theory and practice has been developed at The University of Chicago Graduate School of Business, The Wharton School, Stanford University, The Harvard Business School, and other centers of financial research. The availability of computing power and the application of statistical analysis has made possible a quantum leap in capital market understanding. The work of Harry Markowitz in the early '50s, in particular *Modern Portfolio Theory*, and its offspring have created a framework which has been refined in the crucible of the real world.

Virtually all large funds have adopted the sort of systematic approach which this book will outline. The principles we'll discuss have gained rapid acceptance simply because they work better than other approaches. The old seat-of-the-pants method has been discredited. In large part, some of the recent advances have been driven by the regulatory whip of the Employees Retirement Income Security Act (ERISA) laws.

ERISA has created a framework for the prudent oversight of corporate retirement plans. While ERISA does not govern most endowment and foundation funds, it provides an instructive model. Section 404 of ERISA sets out a standard often referred to as "the prudent expert rule." A plan fiduciary is expected to oversee assets as would "a prudent person *familiar* with such matters." In other words, the good heart, empty head defense doesn't work.

ERISA was signed into law in 1974 in response to the bankruptcy of Studebaker and the loss of pension benefits by the Studebaker employees. The regulation and subsequent litigation have created a set of fiduciary standards which include mandates to prudently: diversify assets, hire investment managers (who become co-fiduciaries), monitor results, and avoid any hint of self-dealing.

To put teeth into ERISA, Congress established *personal* financial liability for any fiduciary breaches. Plan trustees and administrators discovered that improper oversight of plan assets could cost them dearly. Furthermore, Congress mandated that any fines levied could not be guaranteed by the plan or sponsoring company. Such fines can't even be discharged in bankruptcy. These Draconian measures have proven successful in establishing a standard of prudency.

The ERISA model provides a good road map for the oversight of any large pool of money. As a result, foundation or endowment trustees have available a substantial body of theory and practice upon which to draw. This book will lay out a step-by-step approach to sound asset management based upon those principles.

THE DON'TS: PITFALLS TO AVOID

Borrowing from the ERISA model, you probably want to avoid:

- **Doing it yourself**—Unless you or other board members are professional money managers, don't assume that you can generate competitive returns by investing on a part-time basis. Amateurs operating by the seat-of-their-pants cannot hope to outperform professionals armed with state-of-the-art technology and superior information.

- **Market timing**—Study after study shows that no one has been able to time the market well enough to beat the returns on Treasury bills over a prolonged period. There are too many variables. Even if you pick the right time to get out, you're unlikely to get back in. Markets tend to advance in short, explosive rallies; if you miss a few trading days, you may lose most of the return for the year. A University of Michigan study found that in the bull market of the '80s the S&P 500 returned an average of 17.5 percent per year. This was accomplished over approximately 2,500 trading days in that period. However, a "market timer" who missed only the 10 best days saw his return drop to 12.6 percent. If that person missed the 20 best days, the return dropped to an annual 9.3 percent, and if he missed the 40 best days out of 10 years, the annual return was a mere 3.9 percent per year!

- **Placing all your eggs in one basket**—This can cause disaster in two ways. First, inadequate diversification means that you may find yourself holding asset classes which have done well and none of those classes which *will* do well. It's human nature

to load up on last year's winners and avoid last
year's losers. In other words, you buy the expensive assets and avoid the cheap ones. Secondly,
when a fund is over-concentrated, it is often because the trustees are trying to avoid risk. They
may place too much of the fund in bonds or cash
instruments. The result is usually an inadequate
rate of return.

- **Exclusively using the "old boy" network**—Selecting
  financial advisors on the basis of a lending relationship, familiarity, or anything other than expertise is
  not very smart. You have to do a little more work to
  search for a reasonable number of candidates, but the
  effort can be rewarding. The difference in returns
  between winners and losers is enormous.

- **Chasing the hot manager**—Past performance alone
  is not only "not a guarantee of future results," it's
  actually a *bad* predictor of future performance (we'll
  explore some of the reasons why in the chapter on
  style). You have to look deeper to find managers
  who offer a decent shot at success, as explained in
  the chapters on manager search and selection.

- **Not minding the store**—You may have done everything right in allocating assets and selecting managers, but if you fail to monitor and adjust your
  portfolio, you're unlikely to get the results you
  hoped for.

THE DO'S: STEPS TO SUCCESS

Among consultants and other financial professionals, there
is little debate that the following steps represent the essential elements in a sound financial program. The remainder
of the book will elaborate on this outline.

Step 1. Set Goals

The old saw "failing to plan is planning to fail" is nowhere more true than in the investment arena. If you haven't crystallized spending objectives, time horizon, and acceptable risk levels, you will be hard put to avoid the myriad pitfalls which face foundations and endowments. Building investment success is a lot like building a house. You don't set up the bench saw and start cutting two-by-fours before you've drafted the blueprints. And to draft those blueprints you need to clarify what you're trying to accomplish.

Step 2. Allocate Assets

This is arguably the most important step. Virtually every academic study shows that asset allocation is the main contributor to portfolio returns and also is the prime mechanism used to quantify and control risk. The real question isn't, "Should I buy IBM or Compaq?" it's "How much should I put in stocks versus bonds versus cash?" In the past few years, new research has refined this process. Developments such as the use of downside risk or *semi-deviation* have added new dimensions to this important step. If you haven't looked at your asset mix in the past three years, it's probably time to examine it.

Step 3. Develop a Written Investment Policy

If it isn't in writing, it is a wish, not a plan. You wouldn't start a company without a written business plan. In fact, you wouldn't even put a deck on your house without some kind of design. Why then, when it comes to the oversight of millions of dollars, do so many institutions fail to reduce their objectives and strategies to writing? Your investment policy statement is the document that defines the operation of your fund. It contains your written instructions to your money managers.

McDonald's has sold billions of dollars worth of hamburgers. Every single item in the operation of each restaurant is included in its manual. Employees are told exactly how hot to make the grease which cooks the fries and precisely how long a hamburger can sit before it must be discarded. The result is that a group of high school students working part-time can operate a highly profitable restaurant. Apply the same systematic approach to your investment fund and you stand a good chance of winning in the intensely competitive financial arena.

Step 4. Select Managers

Although asset allocation is crucial, selecting above-average managers can potentially add millions of dollars to your fund over a period of years. The trick is, of course, to identify above-average managers before the fact. As we've said, past performance alone is a terrible predictor of future results. We will discuss a process that can potentially identify those characteristics which do have predictive value. The study of manager style has been a fertile area of research. One pioneer has been Professor William Sharpe, Nobel Laureate from Stanford University. He has demonstrated that, at the manager level, style is the key determinant of returns. We'll give you both a process for manager selection in Chapters 9 and 10 and an overview of some of the cutting edge tools available to analyze investment style in Chapter 8.

Step 5. Evaluate Performance

Without an ongoing program to monitor the performance of your investments, you have little chance of success. By performance evaluation, we don't mean a thick book of statistics analyzing each nuance of the portfolio in mind-numbing and unusable detail. Nor do we mean a cursory comparison of the managers' performance to a simple index like the S&P 500. We *do* mean an evaluation of your progress as measured against: (1) your goals, (2) an appropriate benchmark, and (3) a universe of similar managers. This analysis should also take into account the level of risk which led to the returns and the source of over- or underperformance. Effective performance evaluation should answer these two questions: "What does it mean?" and "What should I do?"

Use this book as a reference, if you prefer, by paging ahead to chapters that might be of interest to you, or follow along as we lead you step-by-step through the process. We will provide you with examples and case studies as well as worksheets and forms where appropriate.

3

CHAPTER

Set Goals

Lars peered through the gray mist. The sail was limp, and the waves slapped against the side of the dragon ship. He made another line on the piece of slate with the tip of his iron knife. Twelve days, twelve lines. The men were silent. Two weeks ago, when the sun shimmered on the waves and the wind filled the sails, the men had sung: songs of glory, songs of battle, songs of love and homeland. And at night the three stars of the navigator's triangle twinkled in the black sky, a faint beacon safely leading them westward. Now they were fearful. Without the sun or the stars they were adrift. If they veered north they could perish in an early winter ice storm. If they drifted south they could reach the end of the world. The ancient tales told of the place where the sea poured off the edge of the earth. They said the water falling into the void boiled into a thick mist . . . just like the fog that had engulfed them for the last twelve days!

But Lars was not afraid. He had a secret talisman, given to him by his father. Before that it had belonged to his father's father. As the others napped fitfully, Lars scooped seawater into a wooden bowl. Untying the small leather bag from the cord around his neck, he poured the contents into his hand. He dropped a flat circle of polished wood into the seawater in the bowl. He carefully placed a small rectangular piece of stone on the floating wood. On the stone was scratched an arrow. He stared intently at the bobbing wood. It seemed to turn itself until the arrow pointed toward the prow of the ship. Lars scooped the wood and the rock out of the bowl, threw the water over the side, and placed the items back in the leather pouch.

"Wake up!" he shouted to the helmsman. "We're heading north. Turn the ship."

If you are to chart a successful path for your fund, you need to know where you want to go. You must have a sense of "true north" for your endowment or foundation. Envision what you want to do over the next 10 to 20 years. Only with that picture clearly in mind can you begin to formulate goals. You need to understand and clearly articulate your most central goals. For example, we work with a beneficial society whose members share a common national ancestry. The society has a dual purpose: to help espouse common history, culture, and values, and also to fund and maintain a home for senior citizens. While the first part of the foundation's objectives can withstand some belt-tightening, it would be disastrous if there was a shortfall in the operating funds for the home. To maintain the funding for the home is one of their most central goals.

THE MISSION

As a first step, a board should compose an accurate yet concise articulation of the fund's mission. This necessitates a lot of self-examination. What do you need the money for?

When? Will there be future contributions? Do you need to return principal at some future date? Are annuity trusts involved? Exhibit 3–1 is a worksheet which may help you through this process.

EXHIBIT 3–1

Objectives Worksheet

Organization: _____
Address: _____

I. Mission Statement
    A. Purpose of the fund: _____

_____

_____

    B. Objectives: [for example: to further the purposes of Section A by providing]:
    $_____ (or _____%) for _____;
    $_____ (or _____%) for _____; &
    $_____ (or _____%) for _____]

II. Assumptions
    _____ $ Current value of fund
    _____ % Annual return past 5 years
    _____ % Estimated return next 5 years
    _____ % Inflation

III. Sources
    ▪ Contributions next 5 years $_____
    ▪ Earnings per year $_____ × 5 = $_____
                 Total: $_____

IV. Uses of Funds
    ▪ Spending $_____ per year × 5 = $_____
    ▪ Return of principal in next 5 years = $_____
    ▪ Annuity payments $_____ per year × 5 = $_____
    ▪ Other $_____
                 Total: $_____

Source: DiMeo Schneider & Associates, L.L.C.

EXPECTED RETURN

As the second step, you need to move from the mission statement toward a consensus of how that mission can best be accomplished. You need to translate your goals into a desired rate of return. In fact, when we get to Chapters 5, 6, and 7 (on asset allocation) you'll see that one of the crucial inputs is the return required to meet your objectives. To skip this step is to ensure trouble for your fund. You must carefully consider a number of variables that can affect return, which we will examine in this chapter.

INFLATION

Inflation is the most fundamental factor impacting the return of any long-term fund. Spending must increase at some minimum level over time just to keep up. For example, a national fraternity maintains a scholarship fund to help deserving undergraduate members. A wealthy alumnus more than doubled the size of this fund with a bequest in 1964. At that time, spending was equal to 5 percent of fund assets. However, spending requirements in 1964 were much smaller. A semester's tuition at the University of Illinois was a mere $125 back then! Room and board at the fraternity's Illinois chapter house was $100 per month. As of January 1997, tuition is $2,400 a semester, and room and board is $265 each per month (see Exhibit 3–2). Tuition increased on average 9.67 percent per year! Room and board only inflated 3.1 percent per year. The fund needed an average return of 10.9 percent per year in order to provide the same number of scholarships in 1996 as it did in 1964. This is why you must turn to the capital markets. "Safe" investments like Treasury bills or certificates of deposit have not provided those kind of returns.

Of course, there are additional, unique variables that affect your fund. You must also pay attention to anticipated contributions, established spending patterns, and future

EXHIBIT 3-2

Cost Comparison

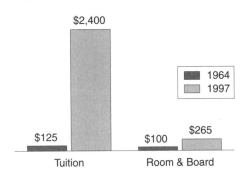

Source: DiMeo Schneider & Associates, L.L.C.

spending growth. Most funds seek to provide for both the present and the future. You need to grow capital for the long-term while providing income in the short-term. Achieving this balance requires careful and prudent planning. A touch of investment wisdom helps as well.

TOTAL RETURN

Out with the old, in with the new. It's time to realize a great truth: A dollar in interest income equals a dollar of capital gains (with some important exceptions, which we'll discuss later). Historically, investors conscious of spending policies have limited their definition of return to dividends and interest. As a result, their investment strategies have focused on the immediate need for income only to neglect capital growth. Meanwhile, the inflation demon inexorably chews away at the real purchasing power of the fund.

In an effort to maximize income, trustees have often forced the fund into a lower total return (see the chapters on asset allocation). Total return simply adds capital gains to the list of potential income sources. Income and growth *can* work together rather than in opposition.

FLEXIBILITY

If you incorporate the total return method into your spending policy, you will be able to consider asset classes and securities in terms of greatest overall return potential, regardless of dividends and interest. The strongest investments may not be the highest yielding. For example, if you invested $100,000 in intermediate U.S. Treasury bonds on January 1, 1970 and reinvested all the interest income, you had $917,751 as of December 31, 1995.[1] But, that same $100,000 invested in Walmart stock grew to $138,084,835! By the way, that number assumes that you spent all the Walmart dividends. Which was the better investment?

Do we hear an objection? "If I invest in a Treasury bond, I know exactly what my income will be. What if I had invested in Pan Am Airlines instead of Walmart? I could have lost everything. Even with a good manager or mutual fund, I might have negative return for a year or even longer!" This is a valid concern. We don't suggest picking one stock. Nor do we suggest a one-year time horizon. However, academic research shows that if you had diversified, maintained a long-term holding period, and periodically rebalanced the portfolio, you'd have produced substantially better results over the past half century than with a portfolio of bonds alone.

The total return approach helps your money managers, too. They will have the much easier task of investing for the maximization of both capital growth and income. They avoid the pitfall of managing for one to the exclusion of the other. When the time comes to allocate gains or losses, they are not constrained by the separation of money into pools (income/spending and gains/capital . . . again, unless there are special trusts as part of the fund).

---

1. Ibbottson Associates, *1996 SBBI Yearbook*, pp. 198–199.

SPECIAL FUNDING

Sometimes gifts to an endowment or foundation take the form of a charitable remainder trust (CRT). Typically this is in the form of an *annuity trust*. A person may gift assets in an arrangement which provides income to the donor and his or her spouse during their lifetimes. The body of the trust passes to the institution after their deaths. In a rarer arrangement, the foundation may receive income from a trust for a certain period of time and then the corpus or body of the trust passes to the donor's heirs. In either case those particular assets must be managed in accordance with the dictates of their trust documents. However, this does not preclude the overall fund from adopting a total return policy. The board merely accounts for the trusts separately while still envisioning the total fund as one pool of assets.

SPENDING

Under the above method, the return can be utilized in various ways. A *set dollar amount* can be withdrawn at fixed intervals. When returns are high this method will build principal; however, you may have to invade that principal when returns are low. Alternatively, withdrawals may be based on a *percentage of return*, e.g., 75 percent of last year's gain. This method eliminates the possibility of invading invested principal but ensures fluctuations in spending amounts. A third possibility is to withdraw a *set percentage* of fund value—for example, 5 percent of fund assets. With this method, you must be certain to set spending policy below the expected return of the fund. Of course, this means that you need a pretty good estimate of what that return may be or (more commonly) you may employ certain "smoothing techniques."

As we said, you need to begin by carefully defining specific income needs and determining what portion of those needs must come from the fund. The following spending/growth equation may simplify the process:

Long-term real growth rate of fund = total return
on assets + rate of gift additions – rate of fund
spending – rate of institutional inflation

The formula assumes your income needs are based on total return and illustrates the relationship between spending and capital growth. A change in the rate of spending necessitates a change in the real growth rate. Once you plug in figures for inflation, contributions, and spending, you can try different total return numbers to determine the fund's rate of capital growth. The growth rate that balances present and future needs implies the rate of return required.

RISK TOLERANCE

Over our many years consulting endowments, foundations, and qualified plans we have worked with literally hundreds of trustees. We are convinced that built into the human psyche is the optimal risk/return trade-off: "10 percent return with no down years!" The only problem is this doesn't exist.

The old adage "nothing ventured, nothing gained" is a truism in the arena of capital market investment. Presence in the markets means risk. You can minimize that risk, but you can't avoid it. Risk and return are directly related; what you lose in one, you gain in the other. The sequitur might be "the more you venture, the more you *potentially* gain," and vice versa. You need to set your goals in light of this trade-off.

Investment risk is often defined as volatility. Price movement (either up or down) equals risk. There are other possible definitions, such as the chance of loss in a given time period. For an endowment or a foundation, a better definition of risk may be "not achieving long-term goals" or "shrinking the fund's *real* value."

Each board member must address such critical questions as: "How will I react to having less than the anticipated return? What is my comfort threshold—not beating inflation? Depleting principal? By how much? Are my personal risk tolerances appropriate for the fund? What will I do in the event of loss?"

You must somehow translate risk tolerance from human terms into a market comparative number. You must temper your desired return based on the amount of risk implied by that return. The higher the risk, the higher the potential return. If you want low risk you must accept a lower return potential. The board's decision regarding risk tolerance will have real effects on both the growth of capital and the availability of income. Exhibit 3–3 is a rather simple test which may help your board members to begin to assess their risk tolerance.

EXHIBIT 3–3

Committee Input Questionnaire

I. General Information

Please assign each item listed below a number between 1 and 4, with 1 being the most important to you. Assign only one number 4, one number 3, etc.

RANK

_____ Cost

_____ Investment performance

_____ Name recognition of investment managers

_____ Flexibility

Which asset classes should we include for modeling purposes? (check all that apply):

_____ Cash equivalents	_____ Mid-size company stocks
_____ Domestic fixed income	_____ Small company stocks
_____ High-yield fixed incom	_____ International equity (stocks)
_____ Global fixed income	_____ Real estate
_____ Large company stocks	

Exhibit 3–3, *continued*

	Strongly Disagree				Strongly Agree
I view myself as risk averse.	1	2	3	4	5
I view myself as aggressive.	1	2	3	4	5
I can accept volatility in order to get higher return.	1	2	3	4	5
If I lost money in a quarter, I would change strategies.	1	2	3	4	5
I prefer steady returns, even if it means that I get little real growth.	1	2	3	4	5

I define investment risk as (check one):

_____ Loss in a quarter.

_____ Not matching inflation.

_____ Not having enough money to meet fund goals.

Starting with $10,000,000, I would change strategies if the fund had a one-year loss of (check one):

_____ −5 percent or $ 500,000.

_____ −10 percent or $1,000,000.

_____ −15 percent or $1,500,000.

_____ −25 percent or $2,500,000.

_____ −35 percent or $3,500,000.

Circle the portfolio with which you are most comfortable.

Annual Return	A	B	C	D	E
Optimistic	9.8 percent	17.5 percent	25.0 percent	32.4 percent	39.9 percent
Expected	6.0 percent	7.8 percent	9.0 percent	10.0 percent	10.7 percent
Pessimistic	2.2 percent	−1.2 percent	−4.9 percent	−8.6 percent	−12.4 percent

The pessimistic scenario represents the lowest expected return likely to occur in any given year. There is a small (5 percent) probability of exceeding the pessimistic or optimistic results. There is a high probability (50 percent +) of achieving the expected results.

Exhibit 3–3, *concluded*

Please indicate any investment funds/managers/firms you would like included in our search:

Funds/Fund Families/Investment Managers

_____

_____

_____

II. Time Horizon

I will judge investment performance over (check one):

_____ 1 year

_____ 3 years

_____ 5 years

Please describe any special funding requirements. _____

_____

_____

_____

_____

III. Expected Returns

1. To meet our objectives over the next five years, we need to achieve a rate of return of _____ percent per year (compounded).

2. Please provide any additional input that you feel we should consider in our recommendations to you. _____

_____

_____

_____

Source: DiMeo Schneider & Associates, L.L.C.

ASSET CLASSES

After you have set return objectives by using the spending/growth equation (which incorporates inflation, spending habits, and contributions), you will have examined the risk tolerance of the fund. As you start to consider asset allocation, you must make decisions about the types of investments which will be allowed into the fund. Will you go beyond the customary stocks, bonds, and cash? What about small company stocks? International? Real estate? There are many possibilities.

You will initially narrow your choices to those that reflect the board's perception of appropriate classes. The initial pass should be as broad as possible. There are facets of the allocation process which are counterintuitive. Sometimes a risky asset plus another risky asset equals a *less risky* portfolio. You will see the balance of risk and return take shape as you model various asset allocations. In Chapter 5, we discuss the process in depth.

TIME HORIZON

The anticipated life of a fund is extremely important. Most funds plan for a very long, if not infinite, time horizon. In such an environment, volatile investments might be quite appropriate. However, a fund faced with imminent spending demands might be forced to maintain a large position in short-term instruments like Treasury bills. A long-term time horizon means that you can ride out the ups and downs of the market. Endowments and foundations typically have the luxury of such long time horizons. A long-term view coupled with a total return spending policy allows your fund to be very tolerant of short-term risk. You can then absorb return fluctuations in the total value of the fund, not in spending amounts.

SUMMARY

The goal-setting process should lead to a successful investment experience. In order to set the objectives for an endowment or a foundation fund, you must tackle several issues:

- The mission of the fund.
- Current spending practices.
- Aspirations for capital growth.
- Ability to tolerate risk.
- Assumed time horizon.

It is crucial that the final decisions on spending policy, desired return, and risk tolerance accurately reflect the funds' long-term goals. If you attain consensus before investing, it is easier to avoid the panic, committee discord, and emotional decision making which can take hold at critical moments in the markets. And, rest assured, there will always be critical moments in the market.

It's much easier to plan your actions and responses before you invest. The next chapter will show you how to translate those plans into a written investment policy statement. This important document formulates the objectives for a successful fund.

4

CHAPTER

Written Investment Policy

OVERVIEW

After you establish goals and develop an investment strategy, it is imperative that you get them down in writing. This document will ensure that the fund has direction and that the integrity of that direction is maintained over the life of the fund. The written policy must have certain key qualities: it must be clear, thorough, and specific. You need to define parameters and goals in measurable terms. Given that you will use it to direct action, the policy should also be flexible enough to be practical.

You may find it useful to conceive of the investment policy as the business plan or the road map that you and your managers will consult along the way. You communicate the board's investment decisions to managers through the investment policy. The policy stipulates the fund's purpose

and objectives as well as return expectations and risk tolerance level. The selected managers must invest accordingly.

You will find it a welcome anchor when organizational changes or market upheaval create stormy seas for the
fund. At such times, the written investment policy pre-
empts emotional reaction. It is much easier to plan for con-
tingencies in advance than in the heat of battle. The written
policy statement is also a convenient tool to help educate
new board members.

CONTENT

The policy will cover a number of topics. It should be organized in a deliberate manner. In general, you should outline
the purpose for each component of the statement. List its
parameters and the parties who have authority and responsibility for each component. A policy statement flows from
your fundamental decisions on spending policy.

Mission

You should begin with an articulation of the fund's mission
and time horizon. When the board first developed the goals
and objectives for the fund, you had to answer some important questions about your purpose. Now you should put
those answers in writing. The mission statement or decla-
ration of purpose sets the stage for all that is to follow. It
provides the big picture. While it is easy to dive into the
nuances of asset allocation or performance measurement
standards, the mission statement provides the "why." It is
impossible to spell out every possible contingency.
Eventually the investment managers or future board members will have to make a decision on a topic that is not
addressed elsewhere in the policy statement. The mission
statement provides a framework for those decisions.

Spending Policy

Include the specific spending requirements of the fund. This sets the stage for the asset allocation and investment policies which are to follow. It will also be very helpful during times when the capital markets are generous. When the tills are full, it's easy to spend. There will always be constituencies within your organization who can find a good use for the "extra money." Spending policy should take into account the long-range goals of the fund and the ebbs and flows of the markets.

Investment Policy

This is the heart of the document. You should enumerate total return objectives for your fund. Set nominal as well as inflation-adjusted targets. Define the asset classes that will constitute the portfolio and spell out the target percentages in each. You also need to define acceptable ranges. For example, you might decide to allocate 10 percent of the portfolio to small-cap stocks, within an acceptable range of 7 to 15 percent.

It is important to consider sub-asset classes, or "style," as well. (We will tackle that topic in greater depth in Chapter 8.) In the example above, of the small-cap allocation perhaps you might allot 4 percent to a growth-style management and 4 percent to a value-style; the remaining 2 percent might be allocated to "micro cap" (companies whose market capitalization is below $100 million).

Risk

The section of the investment policy statement which deals with risk should be quite specific. Many trustees forget the crucial interaction between risk and reward. To set return

objectives without corresponding risk parameters is meaningless. To get a clear image of this type of misconception,
think of the mantra of the financial media: "Most active
managers can't beat the S&P 500 Index."

It's easy to beat the Index . . . if you take enough risk.
If you want double the return of the index, merely buy S&P
500 future contracts using a two-to-one margin. If the market is up 10 percent, you'll be up 20 percent (minus your
cost to carry the position and your transaction costs). Of
course, if the market is down 10 percent, you'll be down 20
percent (plus your cost to carry and your transaction costs).
Since the markets have been up more than down, you
would have "beaten the market" over the past 15 years.
However, the risk/reward trade-off would not have been
very good. You need to spell out how much risk is acceptable. This can be in terms of volatility (standard deviation),
downside risk, beta, or probability of loss. The point is to
set a measurable standard.

Performance Evaluation

Dedicate a portion of your policy to the need to review and
evaluate managers; the board must outline the method and
frequency with which you intend to measure performance.
You should define benchmarks and peer comparisons (see
Chapter 11). You should also establish a procedure for·
reacting to poor performance and potentially implementing change.

Manager Guidelines

The manager guidelines specify the parameters within
which your managers must invest. The guidelines should
also specify desired constraints on investment in individual
securities. For example, are certain securities prohibited, e.g.,

no tobacco stocks? Do you have guidelines for quality and duration of bonds? Are there limits on the size of the investment in any one issue or sector of the market—for example, no more than 5 percent in the securities of a single issuer? Here the board has the opportunity to further delineate the fund's policy on asset allocation and portfolio rebalancing.

Implementation Procedures

How and when will you review the fund's performance? When will you terminate an underperforming manager? Who will decide? What is the role of your consultant? It may be a very good idea to spell out these issues before the inevitable moments of crisis.

An example may well be your best guide. Exhibit 4–1 is an example of a written investment policy statement and the manager guidelines.

EXHIBIT 4–1

Sample Investment Policy Statement

Statement of Investment Policies, Guidelines, and Objectives
Dated April, 1997
ABC University
Endowment Fund

INTRODUCTION

The following investment plan has been adopted by the ABC University Endowment Fund and may be amended as necessary from time to time.

The Investment Policy of the ABC University Endowment Fund has been established to facilitate a clear understanding of their investment policy, guidelines, and objectives between

Exhibit 4–1, *continued*

the committee and the fund's investment managers, including those of funds held for anticipated disbursements. The policy also sets forth the guidelines and restrictions to be followed by the investment managers. It is the intention of this policy to be both sufficiently specific to be meaningful and flexible enough to be practical.

PURPOSE

The ABC University Endowment Fund exists to provide funding for the operation and special programs of ABC University. ABC University is a not-for-profit institution established in 1892 to provide an education in the liberal arts and sciences to qualified candidates. The Endowment Fund will be utilized to establish or maintain programs which are consistent with the aims of ABC University and the Spending Policy found below. Those aims may include, but are not limited to: maintaining a chair for each of the university's educational departments; providing funds for specific research projects approved by the board; and providing scholarships to worthy students.

SPENDING POLICY

The ABC University Endowment Fund will spend between 5 percent and 7 percent of its assets each year. These funds will be spent on programs submitted to and approved by the board of trustees. The Spending Policy shall be implemented with the intent not only to provide funds for the university's immediate aims but also to preserve and grow assets to meet future spending needs.

INVESTMENT POLICY

The ABC University Endowment Fund shall be invested to provide for growth of principal. The fund shall be invested in a diversified portfolio, consisting primarily of common

Exhibit 4–1, *continued*

stocks, bonds, cash equivalents, and other investments which may reflect varying rates of return. The overall rate-of-return objective of the portfolio is a reasonable "real" rate, consistent with the risk levels established by the Finance Committee. The minimum acceptable rate of return over a full market cycle (3 to 5 years) is that which equals or exceeds the assumed spending rate plus the rate of inflation. The trustees have also established a target return objective, which may be changed from time to time but is currently 8.50 percent.

INVESTMENT OBJECTIVES

Risk

The Fund should experience less risk (volatility and variability of return) than that of a custom index made up of the following indices: 35 percent S&P 500, 10 percent Russell 2000, 20 percent Europe, Australia, and the Far East (EAFE), and 35 percent Lehman Aggregate Bond Index.

Return

The total return objective, measured over a full market cycle (3 to 5 years), shall be to outperform the custom index, made up of 35 percent S&P 500, 10 percent Russell 2000, 20 percent Europe, Australia, and the Far East (EAFE), and 35 percent Lehman Aggregate Bond Index by .5 percent (50 basis points) net of fees.

ASSET ALLOCATION

The target asset allocation for the investment portfolio is determined by the finance committee to facilitate the achievement of the Fund's long-term investment objectives within the established risk parameters. Due to the fact that the allocation of funds between asset classes may be the single most important determinant of the investment performance over

Exhibit 4–1, *continued*

the long run, the Endowment's assets shall be divided into
five asset classes as follows:

Class	Maximum Percent	Minimum Percent	Target Percent
Domestic equities	45	25	35
Small-cap equities	15	5	10
International equities	25	15	20
Fixed income	45	25	35
Cash	35	0	0

The actual asset allocation, which will fluctuate with
market conditions, will receive the regular scrutiny of the
finance committee. The finance committee bears the responsibility for making adjustments in order to maintain target
ranges and for any permanent changes to policy.

CASH FLOWS/REBALANCING

New cash flows (contributions) shall be allocated to investment managers by the chief financial officer. As a general
rule, new cash will first be used to rebalance the total fund
in accordance with target asset allocation policy. On an
annual basis, preferably corresponding with the end of a fis-
cal quarter, investment manager accounts should be rebalanced to be in accordance with long-term asset allocation
targets. The purpose of rebalancing is to maintain the
risk/reward relationship implied by the stated long-term
asset allocation targets. This process may result in with-
drawing assets from investment managers who have performed well in the latest year or adding assets to managers
who have lagged in the most recent period. This policy may
necessitate the purchase and or sale of securities, which
might create additional transaction costs to the account and
the recognition of capital losses.

Exhibit 4–1, *continued*

TRANSACTION GUIDELINES

All transactions should be entered into on the basis of best execution (best realized net price). All fees, commissions, and other transaction costs shall be reported as requested by the finance committee.

PERFORMANCE MONITORING

All guidelines and objectives shall be in force until modified in writing. If, at any time, an investment manager believes that a specific guideline or restriction is impeding his ability to implement his process or meet the performance objective, he should present this fact to the finance committee.

Each investment manager's performance will be reviewed quarterly by the finance committee. Investment managers, as requested, will report portfolio holdings and quarterly performance. Additionally, the managers should provide a written update concerning current investment strategy and market outlook at least every quarter. Managers are required to inform the finance committee of any change in firm ownership, organizational structure, professional personnel, accounts under management, or fundamental investment philosophy.

RESPONSIBILITIES OF THE INVESTMENT CONSULTANT

The investment consultant will provide performance measurement and evaluation reporting for each investment manager and/or fund as well as for the total fund(s). Performance will be evaluated relative to stated policy objectives, appropriate benchmarks, and a universe of investment returns appropriate to the investment manager or fund evaluated. Performance will be evaluated over different time periods including the latest quarter, as well as latest one-, three-, and five-year periods. In addition to performance, the consultant

Exhibit 4–1, *continued*

will provide reporting and evaluation regarding the level of risk associated with a manager's performance as well as the manager's consistency and adherence to the specific style which they were hired to implement.

The investment consultant will also report to the committee with the data available on the compliance of a manager or fund to the guidelines of these policies.

MEETING SCHEDULE

Performance reviews will be held on a quarterly basis.

Managers' Investment Objectives and Guidelines
Dated April, 1997
ABC University
Endowment Fund

GENERAL GUIDELINES FOR ALL MANAGERS

The investment managers shall have complete discretion in the management of the assets subject to the guidelines set forth herein.

Mutual funds or commingled funds may be used in any category of investment management. When one is selected, however, it is expected that the fund(s) will, in general, comply with the guidelines set forth herein. No fund may be used without approval of the Trustee. Any exceptions to these guidelines shall be listed in Appendix A—Exceptions to Investment Manager Guidelines.

Cash equivalents may be held in any manager's portfolio at the manager's discretion so long as the securities used comply with the guidelines established for fixed income managers. Managers will be evaluated, however, based upon their performance relative to the appropriate index

Exhibit 4–1, *continued*

benchmark, regardless of the amount of cash equivalents held during any performance measurement period.

Investment managers shall be required to provide quarterly reports. Performance shall be reviewed each quarter with emphasis on mid- to long-term objectives, generally defined as three and five years, respectively.

Implementation: The portfolio will be reviewed on a quarterly basis to assure compliance with the guidelines.

FIXED INCOME MANAGERS

The investment objective for the fixed income segment is to outperform the Lehman Brothers Aggregate Bond Index by 50 basis points per annum net of fees. In addition, each fixed income manager will be measured against the appropriate benchmark for his/her investment style for the duration of the portfolio as well as against an appropriate peer manager universe. It is expected that the manager(s) will meet the fixed income objective established and will consistently provide investment returns placing the fund's performance at least in the second quartile of the appropriate peer manager universe over a rolling three-year period. In addition, the managers will be evaluated over a rolling five-year period with the same minimum expectation.

Certain guidelines for acceptable fixed income instruments, portfolio quality, diversification, and limitations on the use of certain securities are the same for all fixed income managers unless specifically noted within a specific style category. Exceptions to these guidelines will be specifically identified in Appendix A—Exceptions to Policy and accepted by the Trustee.

Fixed Income Instruments

Subject to limitations noted below, fixed income instruments can include U.S. Treasuries and agencies, U.S. and Yankee

Exhibit 4–1, *continued*

corporate bonds, international non-dollar bonds, mortgage pass-through securities (GNMA, FNMA, FHLMC, Savings & Loan, Banks), collateralized mortgage obligations (CMOs), Eurodollar securities of U.S. and foreign issuers, U.S. preferreds and non-convertible adjustable rate preferreds.

Short-term instruments, subject to limitations noted below, can include U.S. Treasury and agency instruments, certificates of deposit and bankers acceptances of U.S. banks, repurchase agreements, Eurodollar CDs, commercial paper, U.S., Yankee, and Eurodollar floating- and variable-rate notes and certificates of deposit, U.S. money market funds, and bank short-term investment funds.

Forward transactions for the purpose of hedging foreign currencies are permitted subject to limitations noted below.

Quality

High-quality issues (Moody's rating of A or better) should be emphasized with a minimum quality rating of Baa and/or BBB at purchase. It is understood that managers will at times purchase securities with ratings as low as BBB in the belief that the security will experience an increase in rating and therefore be beneficial to the portfolio. Lower grade securities are not to be included in the portfolio for the primary purpose of enhancing yield. If a security's quality rating falls below the equivalent of BBB, and the manager continues to hold the security, the manager shall notify the Trustee and state his/her reason for holding the security. The average quality of the portfolio shall be no less than A.

Certificates of deposit issued by a nationally or state-chartered bank, savings association, federal association, a state or federal credit union, or by a state-licensed branch of a foreign bank are permissible, so long as the long-term debt rating of that institution is rated in a category of A or its equivalent or better by two nationally recognized rating services. In addition the issuing institution must have assets in excess of $10 billion.

Exhibit 4–1, *continued*

Diversification

It is also expected, in general, and unless specifically noted in Appendix A—Exceptions to Policy, that fixed income portfolios shall be well-diversified with respect to sector, industry, and issuer in order to minimize risk.

Investments in securities of a single issuer (with the exception of the U.S. government and its fully guaranteed agencies) should not exceed 10 percent of the portfolio.

Duration

It is expected that the portfolio duration of fixed income manager(s) shall be within 25 percent plus or minus of the duration of the benchmark index for each fixed income portfolio.

Limitations

No more than 20 percent of the market value of a fixed income portfolio may be invested in foreign securities (dollar and non-dollar denominated). No more than 10 percent of the market value of the portfolio may be exposed to foreign currency fluctuation; i.e., at least half of the foreign currency exposure must be hedged into U.S. dollars.

Futures and options, as well as forward contracts to hedge currency positions, must be traded on public exchanges and over-the-counter with the 50 largest international and 25 largest U.S. banks in asset size and leading U.S. and foreign brokers and dealers.

At no time will the use of leverage be permitted in fixed income portfolios.

Derivatives

In all cases, the use of derivatives is subject to the same limitations set for cash market securities (including, but not limited to, duration, counterparty credit quality, asset concentrations,

Exhibit 4–1, *continued*

etc.). Any derivatives used must be highly liquid and have an active secondary market.

Derivatives may be used to replicate transactions that the manager would otherwise execute in the cash markets for purposes of reducing transaction costs or affecting shifts in strategy on an interim basis, and shall not be used for the sole purpose of yield enhancement.

Futures and options contracts are permitted for the hedging of foreign currencies.

Investment in collateralized mortgage obligations (CMOs) is permitted, but limited to planned amortization class (PAC) CMOs. No investment in interest only (IO), principal only (PO) or inverse floater CMOs are permitted. In addition, investment should be limited to agency guaranteed collateral; no private CMOs are permitted. The manager should only accept reasonable and prudent prepayment risk, consistent with the stated objectives of their respective portfolios.

Fixed Income Style Objectives

I. Total return fixed income:

The investment objective for the Total Return Fixed Income segment is to outperform the Lehman Aggregate Bond Index by 50 basis points net of fees on an annual basis. It is also expected that the duration of this segment shall be within 25 percent plus or minus of the duration of the Lehman Aggregate Bond Index.

II. Short-term funds for distributions:

The investment objective for funds waiting for distribution is to outperform 90-day T-bills or the Donoghue Taxable Money Market Fund Average net of fees.

EQUITY MANAGERS

The investment objective for the total domestic equity segment is to outperform the S&P 500 by 50 basis points per

Exhibit 4–1, *continued*

annum net of fees over a full market cycle. The performance of each equity manager will be measured against appropriate benchmarks for each investment style as well as against a peer group universe of managed funds. In addition to short-term performance reviews, the managers will be evaluated over rolling three- and five-year periods; each manager is expected to produce investment returns which rank at least in the second quartile versus the peer group over those periods.

Specific portfolio management decisions, including security selection, size, quality, number of industries or holdings, emphasis on income levels, portfolio turnover, and the use of options or financial futures, are left to the manager's discretion subject to standards of fiduciary prudence and the guidelines set forth herein.

Certain guidelines for portfolio diversification as well as on limitations on the use of certain securities are the same for all equity managers unless specifically noted within a specific style category. Exceptions to these guidelines will be specifically identified in Appendix A—Exceptions to Policy and accepted by the Trustee.

Equity Securities

Subject to limitations noted below, investment managers may invest in equity securities listed on the principal U.S. exchanges or traded in the over-the-counter markets, including American Depository Receipts (ADRs).

Convertible securities will be regarded as equity securities within the portfolio.

Diversification

In no case (excepting mutual fund shares) or without waiver by the Trustee shall a single security exceed 5 percent of the market value of the equity fund at cost and 10 percent at market value.

Exhibit 4–1, *continued*

The weighting of each economic sector shall be no more than 100 percent greater than the sector weighting of the market as represented by the S&P 500 or 15 percent, whichever is greater.

I.   Domestic equity—growth:

The investment objective for the Domestic Growth segment is to outperform the Russell 1000 Growth Index by 50 basis points per annum net of fees and the median of a peer universe of managed growth-style equity funds. The percentage not allocated to equities shall be invested in short-term interest bearing securities. Although this is an equity fund, cash may be used to defend principal fluctuations in adverse market conditions. Specific allocation decisions will be left to the discretion of the investment managers. The use of ADRs is permitted, but it is the intent of this segment to be a domestic portfolio.

II. Large-cap domestic equity—value:

The investment objective for the Large Cap Value segment is to outperform the Russell 1000 Value Index by 50 basis points per annum net of fees and the median of a peer universe of managed value-style equity funds. Managers shall be required to provide quarterly reports. The percentage not allocated to equities shall be invested in short-term interest bearing securities. Although this is an equity fund, cash may be used to defend principal fluctuations in adverse market conditions. Specific allocation decisions will be left to the discretion of the investment managers. The use of ADRs is permitted, but it is the intent of this segment to be a domestic portfolio.

III. Small-cap equity:

The investment objective is to outperform the Russell 2000 Index by 50 basis points net of fees and the median of a peer universe of managed small-cap equity funds.

Exhibit 4–1, *concluded*

IV. International equity:

The investment objective for the International Equity segment is to meet or exceed the Morgan Stanley Capital Europe, Australia, and Far East (EAFE) Index net of fees. Hedging of foreign currencies may be allowed.

Source: Canterbury Capital Services.

SUMMARY

Your investment policy statement should not be mere boilerplate. The goals and objectives should be yours. The procedures and guidelines should be a blueprint, referred to by both your committee and your investment managers at critical moments in the oversight of your fund. For instance, when confronted with a new manager or investment strategy, your first question should be, "does it fall within our policy?" If not, you probably want to pass on the strategy, no matter how appealing it is on the surface. One of the great benefits of your policy statement is that it gives you an "out" when you are being solicited for an inappropriate investment: "I'm sorry, but our policy doesn't allow that."

In other words, don't merely copy the language in the sample. Rather, draft a document that will fit your fund.

5

CHAPTER

Asset Allocation

As the previous chapter showed, spending policy is critical to the ongoing success of any endowment or foundation. And by now, prudent trustees have embraced the total return concept.

This chapter and the next two attempt to convey the importance of asset allocation, its dramatic impact on a fund, and a straightforward approach to the process. Along with spending policy, successful asset allocation is essential in achieving your ultimate goal—for the fund to exist into perpetuity.

ASSET ALLOCATION

Every investor wishes for high returns with low risk . . . if only it were so easy. Risk and return are related; high returns require higher risks, and low risk means low returns over time. Asset allocation is the process of optimizing portfolios or funds. *Optimization* means finding the mix of assets with the maximum expected return at a given level of risk. Mean/variance analysis provides the statistical mechanism for portfolio optimization.

How Important Is It?

Academic studies, including the one shown in Exhibit 5–1, confirm that asset allocation accounts for the bulk of a portfolio's investment results. That is, the key decision is how to diversify your fund among asset classes (e.g., stocks versus bonds versus cash). Sector decisions, such as Treasury bonds versus corporate bonds, or specific security decisions, like buying Compaq instead of IBM, have much less impact.

It's extremely important for trustees to understand and control the asset allocation decision. A common mistake is to jump right into investment manager or fund selection. Those decisions should take a back seat to strategic asset allocation.

The process is like building a house. You wouldn't hire carpenters, electricians, and other workers, however well

EXHIBIT 5–1

Determinants of Portfolio Performance

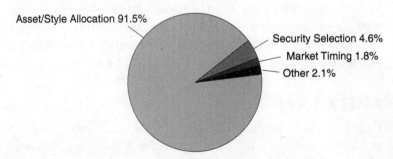

Source: Brinson, Hood, and Beebower, *Financial Analysts Journal.*

qualified, without first developing a blueprint. The spending policy and asset allocation is your fund's blueprint. You and your co-trustees add value by focusing on these key macro issues. You can then hire experts to execute your blueprint.

As consultants, it's not our role to tell you "be conservative" or "be risky." However, it is our job to help trustees gauge their tolerance for risk and create portfolios they can live with. As Exhibit 5–2 indicates, risk itself is not easy to define.

How should trustees define risk? The ultimate goal of most endowments and foundations is to exist into perpetuity. With this objective in mind, trustees are forced to abandon the layman's definition of risk (e.g., the chance of loss in a given year). They need to find an asset allocation which will help them maintain or even expand the fund's principal, over time. Fortunately, trustees have a powerful body of knowledge to draw upon: Modern Portfolio Theory.

EXHIBIT 5–2

Many Different Risks

- Systemic Risk
- Credit Risk
- Knowledge Risk
- Optional Risk
- Market Risk
- Contract Risk
- Interest Rate Risk
- Concentration Risk
- Cross-Market Risk
- Systems Risk
- Raw Data Risk
- Volatility Risk
- Reinvestment Risk
- Basis Risk
- Currency Risk
- Yield Curve Risk
- Limit Risk
- Bankruptcy Risk
- Funding Risk
- Rollover Risk
- Collateral Risk
- Suitability Risk
- Political Risk
- Extrapolation Risk
- Equity Risk
- Accounting Risk
- Hedging Risk
- Legal Risk
- Liquidity Risk
- Commodity Risk
- Capital Risk

Source: ©1995 Capital Market Risk Advisors, Inc.

MODERN PORTFOLIO THEORY

Modern Portfolio Theory (MPT) brings the mathematics of probability theory to the arena of investment management. It postulates the combination of different types of investments in order to produce optimal portfolio results. MPT is based on the collection of data and statistical analysis rather than intuition or the "seat of the pants." As Exhibit 5–3 indicates, there are both efficient and inefficient ways to structure portfolios.

If you could live with the risk (volatility) of Mix A, you'd probably rather be in Mix B (higher return at the same risk level). On the other hand, if you only require the return of Mix A, wouldn't you prefer Mix C (same return with almost no risk)? Mixes B and C are efficient; A is not. In fact, if you plot the portfolio mix with the highest return at each risk level, you will plot an arc. This arc is called the *efficient frontier.*

Obviously, trustees wish to achieve the highest possible return at a given level of risk. Thankfully, the pioneers

EXHIBIT 5–3

Efficient Frontier

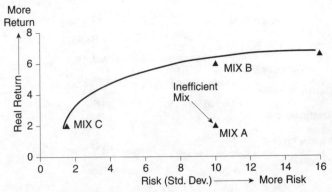

Source: DiMeo Schneider & Associates, L.L.C.

of modern portfolio theory, Harry Markowitz and William Sharpe, have provided a framework which quantifies the trade-offs between risk and reward. Their work, which dates back to the 1950s, has changed the way in which investments are managed. Markowitz and Sharpe received the Nobel Prize in Economic Science in 1990, and today virtually all large pension, endowment, and foundation funds rely on their work.

The essence of modern portfolio theory is that a combination of investments (either asset classes or individual securities) that have a low correlation will enjoy a "smoother path" toward expected returns. For example, consider a pair of stock portfolios. One contains Chrysler and Microsoft, the other Chrysler and Ford. The first portfolio will probably show a greater diversification effect, since the two auto stocks in the second will tend to move in tandem. Owning stocks in two separate industries should reduce risk.

The risk-reduction effect is even further enhanced when the diversification is between asset classes. In Exhibit 5–4, we look at two "risky" assets: large company U.S. stocks as represented by the S&P 500, and foreign stocks as represented by the Morgan Stanley Europe, Australia, and the Far East Index (EAFE). What, do you suppose, would happen if you were to start with a portfolio that was 100 percent U.S. stocks and then changed the mix to 75 percent U.S. and 25 percent foreign? Since you would be starting with a risky asset and adding a riskier asset, intuition tells you that you'd receive higher returns and take on more risk. But that's not the case.

As Exhibit 5–5 indicates, you would actually reduce risk while increasing return. How could this be? U.S. and foreign stocks have low correlation. Put another way, one market "zigs" while the other "zags," resulting in more stable overall returns for the whole portfolio. It may be helpful for you to understand why diversification works this way.

EXHIBIT 5–4

S&P 500 and EAFE Index Asset Allocation
January 1, 1976, to December 31, 1995

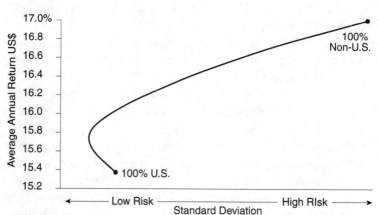

Source: MSCI EAFE Index and S&P 500.

EXHIBIT 5–5

S&P 500 and EAFE Index Asset Allocation
January 1, 1976, to December 31, 1995

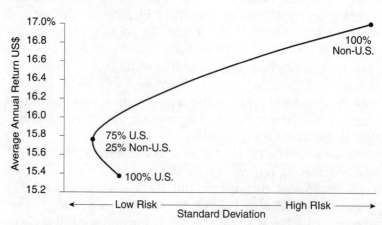

Source: MSCI EAFE Index and S&P 500.

Correlation coefficient is the technical term that describes the relationship between the performance of asset classes. It's one of three elements in the optimization process (the others being *expected return* and *risk*). Correlation coefficients are the most important element in creating an adequately diversified portfolio.

As an example, consider a fund that holds two separate assets: A and B. A and B have prices which rise and fall in tandem. A combination of the two fails to reduce the fund's volatility, or risk. This is perfect *positive correlation*. (See Exhibit 5–6.)

Now assume that you replace asset B with asset C, as in Exhibit 5–7, and that asset C's price moves inversely to that of asset A. A and C are *negatively correlated*. The combination of the two will smooth out the fund's fluctuations.

It's rare to find negative correlation among most asset classes unless you utilize nontraditional (e.g., derivative)

EXHIBIT 5–6

Perfect Positive Correlation

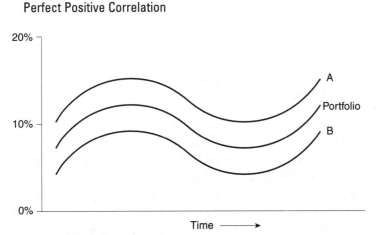

Source: DiMeo Schneider & Associates, L.L.C.

EXHIBIT 5–7

Perfect Negative Correlation

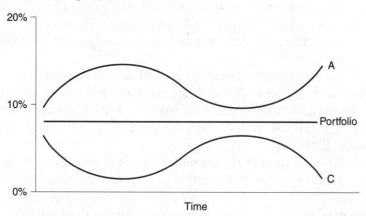

Source: DiMeo Schneider & Associates, L.L.C.

instruments. But even asset classes with low positive correlation provide great diversification. Like pistons in an
engine, different asset classes "fire" at different times to
keep your portfolio running smoothly. Exhibit 5–8 identifies historical correlation between several asset classes.

RISK AND RETURN

Correlation coefficients are one of the three core inputs
used to optimize portfolios. Risk and return must also be
considered.

Risk is often defined as the chance of a bad outcome or
loss. Unfortunately, this definition is not conducive to quantitative evaluation. In financial analysis, standard deviation
is more commonly used. Standard deviation measures the
range of returns relative to the average return. It could be
thought of as the "roller-coaster ride" of quarterly returns.
The lower the standard deviation, the smoother the ride.

As a measure of risk, standard deviation is a component
of mean/variance analysis. Standard deviation is measured

EXHIBIT 5–8

Correlations for Major Asset Classes
From 1926 to 1995

Series	Large Company Stocks	Small Company Stocks	Long-Term Corp Bonds	Long-Term Govt Bonds	Inter-mediate Govt Bonds	U.S. Treasury Bills	Inflation
Large Company Stocks	1.00						
Small Company Stocks	0.81	1.00					
Long-Term Corporate Bonds	0.26	0.11	1.00				
Long-Term Government Bonds	0.19	0.03	0.94	1.00			
Intermediate-Term Government Bonds	0.10	−0.03	0.90	0.90	1.00		
U.S. Treasury Bills	−0.04	−0.09	0.22	0.24	0.50	1.00	
Inflations	−0.02	0.04	−0.15	−0.14	0.02	0.41	1.00

Source: Ibbotson Associates, *1996 SBBI Yearbook.*

as a percentage. In a normal distribution, the return of a portfolio in any given year will lie within a one standard deviation band of the average about two-thirds of the time. In other words, if the mean is 10 percent and the standard deviation is 15 percent, two-thirds of the time the returns will lie between –5 percent and 25 percent (10 percent + or – 15 percent). Returns will lie within a two standard deviation band approximately 95 percent of the time. The familiar, bell-shaped curve in Exhibit 5–9 depicts this example.

Downside Risk

Another important measure, downside risk or *semivariance*, measures the potential loss with respect to a specified target return and may prove quite helpful to trustees attempting to

EXHIBIT 5-9

Probability of Returns

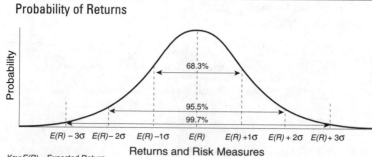

Key: $E(R)$ = Expected Return
σ = Standard Deviation
Source: DiMeo Schneider & Associates, L.L.C.

maintain purchasing power. Downside risk measures the probability and degree of failing to meet the target return. For example, trustees may set a minimum return target of 8.5 percent (5 percent spending + 3 percent inflation + .5 percent administration). They then may want to judge potential allocations within the context of which has the highest probability of exceeding 8.5 percent.

The traditional mean/variance approach may find two portfolios to be approximately equivalent in terms of standard deviation. However, one portfolio may have more downside risk. This can occur when the bell-shaped curve is not symmetrical but rather is skewed to the downside. Unfortunately, the distribution patterns of many asset classes exhibit this skewness.

Expected Returns

The third primary input to portfolio optimization is the *expected return* of each asset class—the operative word being *expected*. Here the adage "garbage in equals garbage out" takes on real meaning.

Obviously, a projection of expected future returns must begin with a look at past results, but which set of returns? Take stocks, for instance. Should you input the past 10 or 15 years of returns? Will the spectacular bull market we've seen "retard" projections? You could use numbers dating back to 1926; however, an argument can be made that our economy and monetary system have changed dramatically, making results from the first half of this century less meaningful. Exhibit 5–10 illustrates the dramatic difference in returns over different time-frames.

While there is no perfect answer to this dilemma, it is our preference to make use of long-term performance figures and then apply some forward thinking. For instance, if stocks have averaged 10 percent for the past 60 years and 20 percent for the last 3 years, odds are that in the coming years, stocks will not continue to grow at double the historic rate.

This chapter has introduced and defined asset allocation. It is one of the most crucial issues you'll address. The next chapter will arm you with an important historical perspective, and Chapter 7 will outline an effective approach to developing an asset allocation strategy for your fund.

E X H I B I T 5–10

Average Annual Returns through 12/31/95

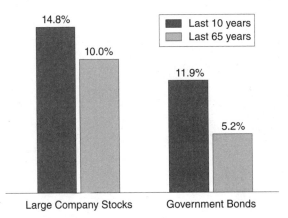

Large Company Stocks   Government Bonds

Source: PIMCO Advisors Funds.

6

CHAPTER

Asset Allocation— Useful Charts and Concepts

We believe:

- Knowledge is power!
- You need information to make informed decisions.
- Informed decisions are generally good decisions.
- Good decisions will help your fund achieve its goals.

In this chapter, we present an outstanding collection of information related to asset allocation. The studies you'll read have been conducted by some of the leading academic and financial institutions. We are grateful for their efforts.

Slowly pore through the pages. Absorb the ideas and challenge your established investment beliefs. Use this information to build your base of knowledge. It will serve you well as you attempt to execute a successful asset allocation strategy for your fund.

EXHIBIT 6–1

Stocks Outperform Over Time
Growth of $1,000, 1946–1995

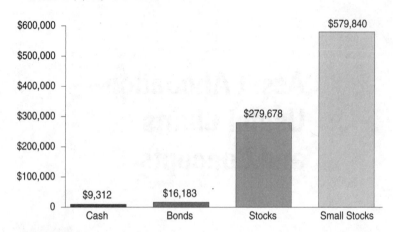

Source: Ibbotson Associates, *1996 SBBI Yearbook.*

EXHIBIT 6–2

But There Are Risks: Some Years Stocks Go Down
Yearly Returns 1946–1995

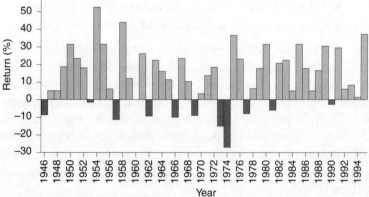

Source: Ibbotson Associates, *1996 SBBI Yearbook.*

EXHIBIT 6–3

Stock Market Risks Are Reduced Over Time
Period 1926–1995

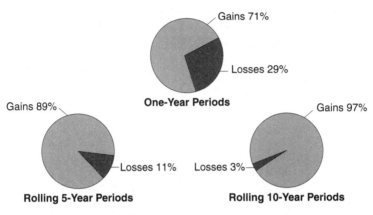

Gains 71%

Losses 29%

One-Year Periods

Gains 89%

Losses 11%

Rolling 5-Year Periods

Gains 97%

Losses 3%

Rolling 10-Year Periods

Source: Ibbotson Associates, *1996 SBBI Yearbook.*

EXHIBIT 6–4

Though Returns Can Still Vary Significantly
Growth of $1,000 1926–1995

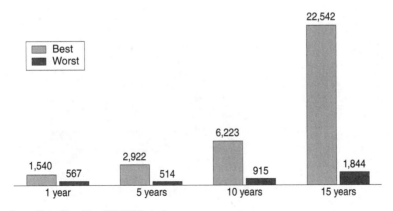

22,542

- Best
- Worst

6,223

2,922

1,540   567   514   915   1,844

1 year   5 years   10 years   15 years

Source: Ibbotson Associates, *1996 SBBI Yearbook.*

EXHIBIT 6–5

And Time Can Compound Poor Allocation Decisions

> So, while time narrows the range of percentage returns, it magnifies dollar differences, notes William Sharpe, a Nobel Prize winner and Stanford University finance professor. With a long holding period, he says, "in one sense risk is less, but in another sense it is more." ▦

Source: *The New York Times.*

EXHIBIT 6–6

Market Timing Is Tough
A Few Wrong Decisions Can Hurt

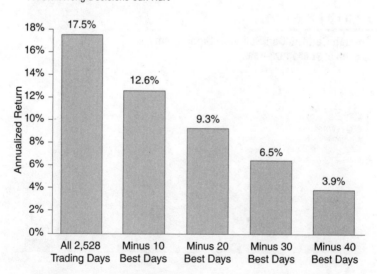

Source: Ibbotson Associates, *1996 SBBI Yearbook.*

E X H I B I T 6–7

Dollar Cost Averaging Beats Timing
$50,000 Annual Investment, S&P 500: 1976–1995

$5,240,540 $6,333,260

Worst Day Each Year   Best Day Each Year
(Market High)   (Market Low)

Source: S&P 500, 1976–1995.

E X H I B I T 6–8

Market Risk Can Be Managed Through Asset Allocation

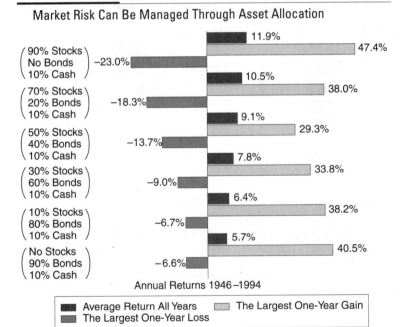

90% Stocks / No Bonds / 10% Cash: −23.0%, 11.9%, 47.4%
70% Stocks / 20% Bonds / 10% Cash: −18.3%, 10.5%, 38.0%
50% Stocks / 40% Bonds / 10% Cash: −13.7%, 9.1%, 29.3%
30% Stocks / 60% Bonds / 10% Cash: −9.0%, 7.8%, 33.8%
10% Stocks / 80% Bonds / 10% Cash: −6.7%, 6.4%, 38.2%
No Stocks / 90% Bonds / 10% Cash: −6.6%, 5.7%, 40.5%

Annual Returns 1946–1994

Average Return All Years   The Largest One-Year Gain
The Largest One-Year Loss

Source: Portfolio Management Consultants, Inc.

EXHIBIT 6–9

And What a Difference Two Percent Make

$10,000,000 Invested for 20 Years at:

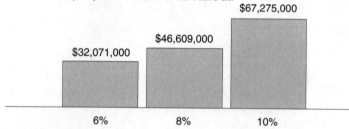

	$67,275,000
$46,609,000	
$32,071,000	

6%   8%   10%

Source: DiMeo Schneider & Associates, L.L.C.

EXHIBIT 6–10

It's a Big World AND the U.S. Is Just One of the Majors

World Equity Markets

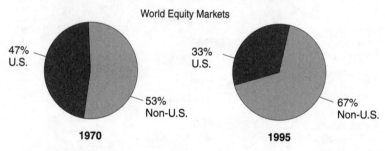

47%
U.S.

33%
U.S.

53%
Non-U.S.

67%
Non-U.S.

1970   **1995**

Source: MSCI.

EXHIBIT 6–11

And Many of the World's Largest Companies Are Overseas

In Fact ...

⟶ 7 of the 10 Largest Auto Companies

⟶ 8 of the 10 Largest Airlines

⟶ 10 of the 10 Largest Banks

... Are Outside the U.S.!

Source: *Financial Times,* January 1996.

EXHIBIT 6–12

Best Stock Markets 1986–1995

It's a Big World II...

The U.S. can't always be on TOP!

Stock Market Performance 1986-1995

	#1	#2	#3
1995	Switzerland 45.03%	U.S. 37.58%	Sweden 34.07%
1994	Finland 52.48%	Norway 24.06%	Japan 21.62%
1993	Hong Kong 116.70%	Malaysia 110.01%	Finland 83.16%
1992	Hong Kong 32.30%	Switzerland 18.10%	U.S. 7.67%
1991	Hong Kong 49.52%	Australia 35.62%	U.S. 30.55%
1990	U.K. 10.29%	Hong Kong 9.18%	Austria 6.70%
1989	Austria 104.85%	Germany 47.06%	Norway 46.12%
1988	Belgium 55.37%	Denmark 53.74%	Sweden 49.38%
1987	Japan 43.18%	Spain 37.85%	U.K. 35.09%
1986	Spain 123.14%	Italy 109.41%	Japan 99.72%

Source: MSCI EAFE Index and S&P 500. Performance is in U.S. dollars, with dividends and capital gains reinvested.

E X H I B I T 6–13

Global Investing Has Lowered Risk
January 1, 1976, to December 31, 1995

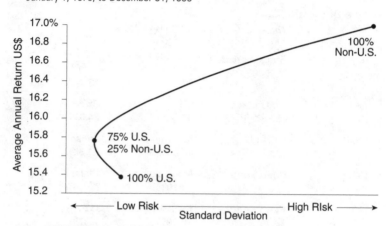

Source: MSCI EAFE Index and S&P 500.

E X H I B I T 6–14

Higher Highs and Higher Lows from a Blended Investment
The Range of High and Low Average Annual Returns 1970–1995

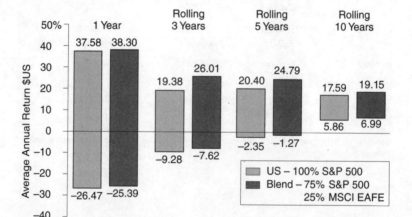

Source: Morgan Stanley Capital International Europe, Australia, Far East (MSCI EAFE) Index and Standard
& Poor's 500 Composite Stock Price Index. Performance is in US dollars, with dividends and capital gains
reinvested.

E X H I B I T 6–15

Real Estate Investment Trusts Outstanding Long-Term Results
Annualized Returns, 20 Years Ending September 30, 1996

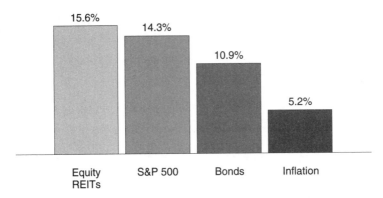

Source: Cohen & Steers, Inc.

E X H I B I T 6–16

And More Diversification
Correlation to S&P 500 Measured by R-Squared

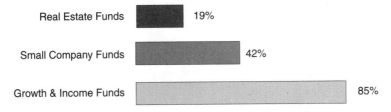

Source: Morningstar, Inc.

7 CHAPTER

Asset Allocation—
The Art and Science
of Implementation

In the two previous chapters we defined asset allocation and the important role it plays in the success of your fund. We also armed you with historical information that will prove useful as you make allocation decisions.

We'll now show you how to implement an asset allocation strategy. It involves both art and science. Few investors, including most consultants, truly understand this concept. On the one hand, you've got an enormous amount of statistical data (science). On the other, you have more "touchy, feely" issues like risk tolerance or asset class preference. Keep this in mind as we proceed.

Exhibit 7–1 identifies your two primary sources of input: capital market assumptions and the trustees' or investment committee's preferences. There is great interplay between these components.

EXHIBIT 7–1

Asset Allocation Strategy

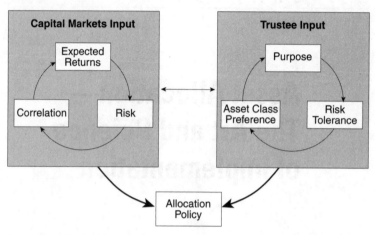

Source: DiMeo Schneider & Associates, L.L.C.

CAPITAL MARKET INPUT

Chapter 5 discussed Modern Portfolio Theory and defined the components used to optimize, or efficiently mix, portfolios. We will briefly recap the three here:

> *Correlation coefficient* measures the mutual variation between two securities or asset classes. Correlation coefficient values may range from –1 to +1. A value of +1 indicates perfect *positive* correlation and therefore no diversification benefit. A value of –1 indicates perfect *negative* correlation (outstanding diversification). A value close to 0 indicates noncorrelation.

> *Practical Points*
> - Historical correlation coefficient data does seem to have predictive value.
> - Negative correlations between asset classes are extremely rare.

Risk is generally defined as the chance of a bad outcome or loss. In financial analysis, standard deviation, which measures the range of returns relative to the average return, is the most popular risk measure.

Practical Points

■ Historical standard deviation data seems to have predictive value.

■ Trustees must also consider the risk of failing to achieve a minimal acceptable return.

■ Trustees can also evaluate downside risk or *semideviation*.

Expected return is the anticipated average return on the asset classes you wish to own. This is a *forecast*.

Practical Point

■ Historical return data is generally thought to have little predictive value.

We've briefly recapped the capital market inputs—correlation coefficients, risk, and return; don't minimize their importance.

OPTIMIZATION

The three inputs listed above are processed in a computer program called an optimizer. While such computer programs provide valuable assistance to trustees and consultants alike, you can get bizarre output if you're not extremely thoughtful about the input.

Remember that these are *forecasting* tools. Beware of blindly assuming that past returns will continue (especially returns of the recent past). For example, assume it's January 1987. High-yield (junk) bonds have enjoyed five years of outstanding performance. In fact, for this period junk bonds produced an average annual return of 20 percent, nearly 15 percent higher than the previous 10-year average.

If you were to optimize a portfolio using those recent returns, you would *overallocate* to that class. Exhibit 7–2 compares the difference in "optimized allocations" using recent rather than historical returns for junk bonds. As you can see, you would end up with a much higher allocation to junk bonds if you assumed that future returns would match those of the recent past. Unfortunately, history did not repeat itself. Exhibit 7–3 shows the actual returns on junk bonds for the years preceding and following the allocation decision.

We are not saying that long-term data is always the most appropriate. We do, however, want to caution you against the classic rookie mistake of extrapolating stellar recent performance into the future.

Consider an absurd example. There was a huge increase in the number of Elvis impersonators between the mid 1960s and late 1970s. That fact makes sense, right? However, it doesn't make sense to extrapolate that dramatic growth into the future. It is very unlikely that by the year 2020, every second person in America will be an Elvis impersonator. The moral: Be thoughtful about your inputs.

Capital market inputs are only half of what you'll need to develop an asset allocation strategy. Let's take a look at what the trustees must provide.

EXHIBIT 7–2

Optimized Portfolios

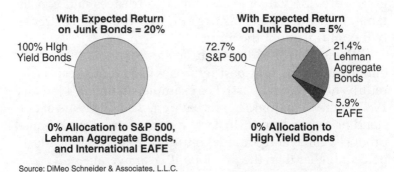

With Expected Return on Junk Bonds = 20%
100% High Yield Bonds
0% Allocation to S&P 500, Lehman Aggregate Bonds, and International EAFE

With Expected Return on Junk Bonds = 5%
72.7% S&P 500
21.4% Lehman Aggregate Bonds
5.9% EAFE
0% Allocation to High Yield Bonds

Source: DiMeo Schneider & Associates, L.L.C.

EXHIBIT 7–3

American Express Financial Advisors
Low Grade Bond Index

Before Allocation Decision		After Allocation Decision	
1982	36.6%	1987	6.5%
1983	13.9%	1988	13.6%
1984	10.7%	1989	0.4%
1985	24.9%	1990	(6.4%)
1986	15.6%		

Source: DiMeo Schneider & Associates, L.L.C.

TRUSTEE INPUT

The trustees' collective input will have a dramatic effect on the long-term results of a fund. Trustees should be serious about this responsibility, and fortunately most are. While they may not always have a great deal of experience and knowledge in the area of asset allocation, trustees should, at a minimum, understand the data that is required of them. Let's look at each component.

Policy

The policy incorporates the background, purpose, and mission of the fund, including its *time horizon*. Is the fund, like most endowments and foundations, intended to exist indefinitely? Or rather, was it established to achieve some specific short- or intermediate-term goal?

Spending targets are equally crucial. We must address the hows and whys of spending along with future needs (e.g., to increase the number of scholarships by a third over the next 10 years).

Finally, trustees must respect any restrictions that donors have placed on funds. Trustees may also establish their own restrictions.

Chapter Seven

Asset Classes

With well-defined objectives, trustees can determine which
asset classes make sense. Of course, this process should
begin with an examination of the fund's existing holdings.
Which asset classes are represented? Which might be inappropriate given the fund's objectives and restrictions? To
address these and similar questions, it may be helpful to
review Exhibit 7–4, which defines major asset classes and
presents historical return and risk measures for each.

The trustees at this point are not asked to determine
intuitively which asset classes might efficiently work
together to produce superior results. Rather, they should
identify those asset classes they will allow to be optimized
and those they wish to exclude.

It is better to include as many asset classes as possible.
We suggest that you initially eliminate only those classes in
which you cannot invest. In other words, exclude investments

E X H I B I T 7–4

Historical Return/Risk

Index	Description	10-Year Avg. Annual Return Ending 10/96	10-Year Stand. Dev. Ending 10/96
S&P 500	Large Company Stock	14.65%	14.29%
S&P 400	Mid Company Stock	15.00%	15.92%
Russell 2000	Small Company Stock	11.30%	18.20%
Wilshire REIT	Real Estate Stock	6.44%	13.00%
MSCI EAFE	International Stock	9.61%	18.12%
MSCI World	Global Stock	11.43%	14.53%
LB Aggregrate	Total Bond	8.57%	4.50%
LB Long Gov/Corp	Long-Term Bond	9.66%	7.95%
LB Inter. Gov/Corp	Intermediate Bond	7.97%	3.49%
T-Bill	U.S. Treasury Bill	5.48%	0.47%
CPI	Inflation	3.58%	0.71%

Source: Mobius Group, Inc.

that would violate your policy. Also exclude those that you may be permitted to own but for practical reasons simply cannot purchase. For example, a $3 million foundation probably can't invest in venture capital as an asset class because of the generally high minimum purchase requirements.

Risk Tolerance

Risk is a difficult concept. When we ask investors for their definition of risk, the response we hear most is "losing money." As we probe, we find out that they mean a short-term decline in the value of the investment. With this definition of risk, it's understandable that investors would view stocks as risky and cash and bonds as less risky.

But is this the appropriate definition of risk? What about achieving a negative return after inflation? This is the risk of shrinking your fund's real value, and thus spending, over time. As Exhibit 7–5 illustrates, inflation can wreak havoc on your fund's value.

Exhibit 7–6 provides a helpful risk tolerance questionnaire that can be used to take the pulse of an investment committee. Remember, the asset allocation process is both art and science; this questionnaire can help to get things rolling.

EXHIBIT 7–5

Growth of $1.00
1926–1995

	Before Inflation	After Inflation
Small Company Stocks	$3,822	$446
Large Company Stocks	1,114	130
Government Bonds (long-term)	34	4
Treasury Bills	13	1.50

Source: Ibbotson Associates, *1996 SBBI Yearbook.*

EXHIBIT 7–6

Risk Tolerance Assessment

Name: _____

I. General Information	Disagree				Agree
I view myself as risk averse.	1	2	3	4	5
I view myself as aggressive.	1	2	3	4	5
I can accept volatility in order to get higher return.	1	2	3	4	5
If I lost money in a quarter, I would change strategies.	1	2	3	4	5
I prefer steady returns, even if it means that I get little real growth.	1	2	3	4	5

I define investment risk as (check one):

_____ Loss in a quarter.

_____ Not beating inflation.

_____ Not having enough money to meet our goals.

Starting with $1,000,000, I would change strategies if I had a one-year loss of (check one):

_____ $50,000   (Down 5%)

_____ $100,000 (Down 10%)

_____ $150,000 (Down 15%)

_____ $250,000 (Down 25%)

_____ $350,000 (Down 35%)

Circle the one portfolio with which you are most comfortable.

Average Annual Return

Scenario	A	B	C	D	E
Optimistic	9.8%	17.5%	25.0%	32.4%	39.9%
Expected	6.0%	7.8%	9.0%	10.0%	10.7%
Pessimistic	2.2%	−1.2%	−4.9%	−8.6%	−12.4%

The Pessimistic Portfolio represents the lowest expected return likely to occur in any given year. There is a small (less than 5%) chance that the loss could be greater in any year.

II. Time Horizon

I will judge investment performance over (check one):

_____ 1 year

_____ 3 years

_____ 5 years

Source: DiMeo Schneider & Associates, L.L.C.

IMPLEMENTATION

We've now identified two separate sets of inputs that will be used to produce potential allocation strategies. Once different asset allocations are created, trustees must ultimately choose one for their fund. Exhibit 7–7 summarizes the process in chronological order.

Two new concepts, sub-asset class allocations and rebalancing, are introduced in Exhibit 7–7. Let us define each.

Sub-asset class allocations are made on the basis of style or market capitalization. Generally you want to optimize, considering only broad asset classes. For example, we would not seek to model the allocation between large company domestic *growth* stocks and large company domestic *value*

EXHIBIT 7–7

The Asset Allocation Process

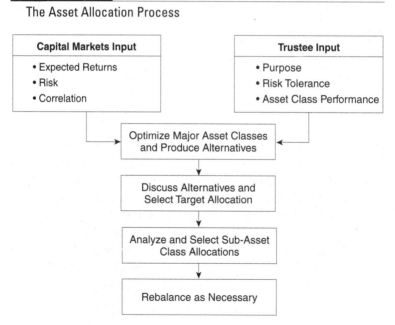

Source: DiMeo Schneider & Associates, L.L.C.

stocks. A computer will inappropriately overweight one style based on very modest differences in the inputs used.

It's better to optimize for major asset classes, and then "fund" each class by blending the appropriate sub-asset classes. Generally you'd like the portfolio to be style neutral, or balanced between growth and value. Your first step might be to determine what percentage of the fund should be allocated to large company stocks. Although ultimately you desire an equal weighting of growth and value style, your initial funding might not be equal. If, for instance, growth style investing has substantially outperformed value investing for a two- or three-year period, and growth stocks appear to be overpriced, you may wish to initially underweight growth and overweight value.

Let us emphasize that the amount of over- or underfunding should be modest. You can't time the market but you can be thoughtful in your allocation of dollars.

REBALANCING

Market performance will cause the fund's actual allocation to drift from your target over time. You should be prepared to occasionally rebalance. The questions are, when and how?

There are several answers. Some funds rebalance at specific time intervals—quarterly or annually—while others rebalance when the actual allocation moves outside a predetermined range. For example, trustees might have a target allocation of 20 percent to small company domestic stocks with upper and lower limits of 15 percent and 25 percent, respectively. If market action caused the small-cap allocation to hit, say, 28 percent, the trustees would need to rebalance.

Again, you can't time the market. Rebalancing ensures that the fund maintains the return and risk characteristics that the trustees originally intended. If an asset class becomes overweighted through outperformance, those characteristics will change.

SUMMARY

Asset allocation is the single largest determinant of investment results. Developing a successful allocation strategy requires that trustees appreciate and understand the importance of their role. Combined with thoughtful capital market assumptions, trustee input can produce a successful asset allocation strategy. In other words, returns can be maximized at a given level of risk.

In the next chapter, we address style analysis and the important role it plays in the asset allocation of your funds.

8
CHAPTER

Style

It was the same as before. The digital readout blinked, flashing like the red neon sign on a cheap motel. The seconds ticked backwards toward zero as his shaking fingers punched in numbers on the keyboard. "ACCESS DENIED" flashed on the screen. A drop of sweat zigzagged down his forehead and slithered along the side of his nose before falling to the top of the device. There was something he should remember, something very important. It was right at the edge of his consciousness. Why couldn't he think clearly? Agent Kevin McIlvie knew that there was a pattern, if only he could recall it.

Each flash of the readout bathed his face in a hellish glow. Red highlights glistened on his forehead and cheeks. Somewhere a warning horn began to bray; the sound was synchronized with the flashing numbers.

He glanced up. The somber walnut paneling of the confer-ence room looked threatening rather than substantial in the mechanical flicker. "What am I missing?" Each blast of the horn now seemed timed with the pounding of the arteries in his neck. Twelve seconds. The blaring horn was replaced with a female voice. "You have five seconds . . . four seconds . . . three seconds . . . two seconds . . . one second."

Kevin snapped awake. He was in his study. The manager search report had fallen from his hand and was lying on the car-pet. He took a deep breath. He must have dozed off. Then he remembered; he'd had that same dream three years ago, the last time they'd changed managers for the fund.

How could they have this run of bad luck? They'd had such high hopes for each of their investment managers. Each one had enjoyed a terrific track record . . . until they started working for the foundation! The managers were obviously smart people. They'd all come with the highest recommendations, but somehow, as soon as they were hired, their performance began to fall apart. Maybe Larry Smith was right. Maybe performance was nothing but luck. Maybe the foundation should give up and just buy an index fund. But there seemed to be a pattern; if only he could see it.

It's an old story. After two or three years of underper-formance, the board throws in the towel and votes to replace the investment manager. So you start the search process all over again. You begin to keep and review the solicitations which show up in your mail almost daily. You ask friends who sit on other boards for their recommenda-tions. Maybe you buy a copy of *Nelson's Directory of Investment Advisors* and begin to look at the rankings. Your broker offers a name or two, and, of course, the other board members have recommendations as well. You develop a list of four finalists and invite them in.

Each presentation is terrific! The money managers bring glossy, color brochures; they describe in detail their philoso-phy and procedures, as well as buy and sell disciplines. They use slick computer graphics and LCD projectors to make their points. And it goes without saying that their investment performance is outstanding. Over the past one-, three-, and five-year periods each investment advisor has substantially beaten the market. After prudent deliberation the board selects the new manager.

So, what's wrong with this process?

Nothing, except that it's exactly what you did to select the manager you've just fired. While seemingly logical and thorough, the process leaves out a crucial element . . . style!

STYLE ANALYSIS

Recent academic research shows that a manager's investment style is crucial to his or her performance. What do we mean by style? Are we talking about the way the managers dress or speak? Do we refer to their interpersonal skills? No! By style we mean something about the kind of stocks or bonds a given investment advisor purchases and the process he or she went through to select those securities.

Growth versus Value

Think of the universe of equity managers. Approximately half that group could be classified as *growth-style* investment advisors. Growth managers seek out companies with rapidly growing earnings. The idea is that rising earnings ultimately mean a rising stock price. If you can identify a Microsoft or Wal-Mart at an early stage, it almost doesn't matter what you paid for the stock. After a few years of 20 percent-plus earnings growth, the stock price will have doubled or tripled. Obviously that style works.

A different approach is followed by a *value-style* manager. He or she doesn't necessarily seek fast-growing companies. Instead the value manager focuses on price. In fact, another name for the value style is "price-driven." The value manager does not necessarily buy companies with rapid earnings growth. Often he or she will purchase a stock when some bad news has driven down the price. The idea is to buy a dollar's worth of assets for 50 cents. The manager believes that eventually the undervalued stock will come back into favor and once again be priced at a hundred cents on the dollar. The value approach also works.

However , growth and value are rarely in vogue at the same time. Exhibit 8–1 shows the fluctuation of the Wilshire Growth and Value indices over a 15-year period. The horizontal center line represents the performance of the S&P 500 index over that time. You can see that when growth stocks outperform, value stocks tend to lag, and vice versa. This flip-flopping of the favored style is at the root of many manager selection problems. In 1991, after a three-year period in which the average growth-style manager outperformed the average value manager by 6.2 percent per year, record numbers of outstanding value managers were given the sack.[1] Unfortunately, long-suffering trustees often replaced excellent value managers with mediocre growth-style advisors. What happened in 1992? You guessed it, the

EXHIBIT 8–1

Benefits of Investment Style Diversification
Diversification of Style Reduces Total Fund Risk

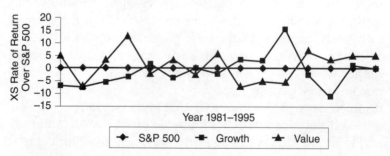

Source: DiMeo Schneider & Associates, L.L.C.

---

1. Data source, Mobius Group, Inc.

average value manager beat the average growth manager by 4.0 percent![2] This alternation of favored investment styles goes a long way toward explaining why "past performance is no guarantee of future results."

Variations

There are subsets of the two major styles. Growth managers may be "traditional growth" managers as described above, or they may be "earnings momentum" players. That is, they may be looking for companies where the rate of growth is accelerating. They may look at "earnings surprise" (companies which report earnings above analysts' estimates not only tend to go up in price, they also tend to repeat the positive surprise). There are even those who call themselves "growth at a reasonable price" (GARP) managers. They look not only at a stock's growth characteristics but also at valuation criteria. These and other subsets comprise the growth style.

Value-style managers come in many varieties as well. There are traditional value managers as originally described. There are also "contrarian" investment advisors. They bet that the majority is generally wrong; if a stock is shunned by other managers, it usually has no place to go but up. There are also those who try to estimate the "private market value," or the price an informed buyer would pay for the whole company. Value managers spend a lot of time looking at a company's balance sheet. They want to find out if there are overlooked assets (for example, land bought in 1900 and carried on the books at the original purchase price). They also look at valuation measures like stock price divided by earnings (PE); price-to-sales (the stock price divided by sales per share); price-to-book (price divided by book value); and dividend yield.

---

2. Ibid.

Just to add to the confusion, there are also *core* managers. A core manager buys companies without extreme growth or value characteristics. This type of manager stakes out a middle ground.

Size

Style also encompasses the size of the companies in which a manager invests. For example, an advisor may invest in companies whose market capitalization is larger than $5 billion. Market capitalization means the number of shares of stock outstanding times the price per share; in other words, the total value of the company. A market cap (capitalization) of greater than $5 billion is generally regarded as *large cap*. A market cap between $1 billion and $5 billion is regarded as *mid cap*, and a company whose size is below $1 billion is called *small cap*. Over the long run, small-cap stocks have had higher returns and greater volatility than large-cap stocks.

These distinctions are important because each of the different capitalization segments has their day in the sun. Sometimes small-cap stocks outperform, and sometimes large-cap stocks do. These periods of over- and underperformance can be quite lengthy. From 1983 until 1990, small-cap stocks lagged their large-cap brethren. Then small caps outperformed until the end of 1994.

At any given point in time, a large-cap growth manager could be expected to have a very different performance from that of a mid-cap core manager or a small-cap value manager, and so on. It's no wonder that performance alone is such a terrible predictor of future returns!

Fixed Income Styles

There are also distinct market segments in the fixed income (bond) arena. The type of issuer defines one dimension of fixed income investment style. Managers might invest in bonds issued by the U.S. government, government agencies like Government National Mortgage (Ginnie Mae), quasi-governmental agencies like the Federal National Mortgage Co. (Fannie Mae), municipal governments (cities, states, counties, etc.), or corporations like GE or IBM. There is even a "high-yield" classification, a euphemism for bonds with ratings below investment grade. Below investment grade means that the bonds are ranked below Baa by Moody's, Inc., or BBB by Standard & Poor's; these are also referred to as "junk bonds." The fixed income categories also tend to alternate periods of over- or underperformance.

Duration

Another important dimension of fixed income style is the duration of the bonds purchased. *Duration* measures the sensitivity of a bond's price to changes in interest rates. Average maturity is a key component of duration (there are also other components, such as the stated interest rate or *coupon* and whether the bond is priced at a premium or discount). *Broad* fixed income managers may purchase bonds with maturities of 7 to 10 years or longer. *Intermediate* managers look for bonds with 5- to 10-year average maturities. *Low-duration* managers generally invest in securities with maturities under 5 years.

Average maturity is very important. In periods of rising or falling interest rates, bonds with longer maturities have greater price changes than do short-term bonds. For example, in 1994 long-term U.S. government bonds had a total return (price change plus interest earned) of *negative* 7.8 percent. Intermediate U.S. government bonds lost only 5.1 percent.[3]

Who cares? Why should you be concerned about style? Because knowledge of a manager's style will tell you an awful lot about his or her performance. In fact, style is the single greatest determinant of return at the *manager level!* In

---

3. Ibbotson Associates, *SBBI 1995 Yearbook.*

1988, Nobel laureate William Sharpe, professor of finance at Stanford University, published his initial research regarding the impact of style on manager performance. His studies indicated that over 90 percent of a manager's performance track record was attributable to style![4] And by the way, the difference in performance in any given year can be huge. In Exhibit 8–2, we see that in 1987 the difference between the best- and worst-performing styles was 20 percent!

Two problems: How do you really know the manager's style, and how can you tell if he or she is skillful?

To truly judge a manager's style, can you rely on his or her marketing material? Manager A calls his style "growth." He purchases such stocks as Abbott Labs, Citicorp, General Electric, and Walt Disney Co. Manager A's 1995 performance was 32.3 percent. Manager B also calls her style "growth." She invests in companies like American Express, Anheuser-Busch, PepsiCo, and Time Warner. In 1995,

EXHIBIT 8–2

Spread between Minimum & Maximum Returns by U.S. Equity Style

	Large Growth	Large Value	Mid- Growth	Mid- Value	Small Cap	Hi-Lo Spread
1987	7%	4%	-3%	-5%	-13%	20%
1988	11%	20%	13%	20%	20%	9%
1989	34%	25%	32%	21%	29%	12%
1990	1%	-2%	-4%	-9%	-10%	11%
1991	42%	26%	52%	30%	50%	26%
1992	5%	9%	7%	14%	13%	9%
1993	2%	16%	11%	17%	19%	17%
1994	0%	-1%	-1%	-1%	-3%	3%
1995	36%	30%	37%	26%	30%	11%

Source: DiMeo Schneider & Associates, L.L.C.

4. William F. Sharpe, "Determining a Fund's Effective Asset Mix," *Investment Management Review,* November/December 1988, pp. 56–59.

Manager B returned 29.3 percent for her clients. Manager C also calls himself a growth manager, yet he purchases stocks such as Ames Financial Corp., Cincinnati Bell, National Education, and Zoltek Companies. His 1995 performance was 43.8 percent.

How can you judge between them? Which one is truly the "growth" manager? A talk with each manager only confuses you more. Manager A says, "Over time our stocks produce predictable earnings growth; this ultimately translates into higher stock prices." This manager's five-year performance has been 12.9 percent per year.

Manager B says, "We don't overpay for good growth companies. Our portfolio's price/earnings ratio is only 1.1 times that of the S&P 500, but our growth rate is two times that of the market. When markets get hit we don't lose as much. Our five-year performance is 11.8 percent per year."

Manager C describes himself as "very quantitative." He says, "We calculate modern portfolio theory statistics for individual stocks. We choose those with the highest excess return or *alpha*." This manager has returned 17.7 percent per year for the past five years.

The second problem is determining if the manager is skillful, or merely enjoying a period when his or her particular style is in synch with the markets. Such dilemmas would be solved if you could calculate a specific benchmark which would be appropriate for each manager. Fortunately such tools have been developed; *style analysis* allows you to more accurately determine a manager's approach and also to measure his or her skill against a true benchmark.

PORTFOLIO-BASED STYLE ANALYSIS

The first attempts to gauge an advisor's style were time consuming and complex, but they pointed the way. Stocks were sorted on the basis of characteristics such as P/E, price-to-book ratio, dividend yield, historical earnings growth, and forecast earnings growth. These characteristics became elements in *multifactor models.* "Value" stocks might be assumed to have low P/E ratios, high P/B ratios, and relatively high dividend yields. "Growth" stocks generally have higher historical and forecast earnings growth rates and, often, higher P/Es and lower dividends. A manager's portfolio was examined to see which types of stocks he or she held. To reiterate, the same sort of comparisons can be made based on market capitalization. By examining the holdings in a particular portfolio, you could make some judgments about a manager's style . . . at that point in time. You might determine that "Manager X was a small-cap value manager as of 12/31/96."

This process was clearly an improvement in terms of understanding a manager's investment approach. However, there are several drawbacks. First of all, a great deal of subjectivity is involved. For example, is General Electric a growth or a value stock? Depending on how one weights the criteria, it can be classified as either. As we said, this type of portfolio analysis is time consuming and very expensive.

In essence, you need to analyze the portfolio holdings at least quarterly. And to be thorough you should track every transaction to ascertain that the manager has not changed his or her spots through quarter-end "window dressing." Furthermore, this sort of analysis does not lend itself to historical study since it is often impossible to verify which stocks were held at earlier points in time.

RETURNS-BASED STYLE ANALYSIS

In a 1992 research paper, Professor Sharpe proposed a methodology to analyze a manager's style based on his or her returns. In essence, Sharpe suggested regressing the manager's performance against the performance of pure

indices: *large growth, large value, mid-cap,* and *small stock.*[5]
These have since been modified to: *large growth, large value,
small growth,* and *small value* (see Exhibit 8–3). The four
indices become the four corners of a "map." By means of

E X H I B I T   8–3

Manager Style
September 1991–September 1996

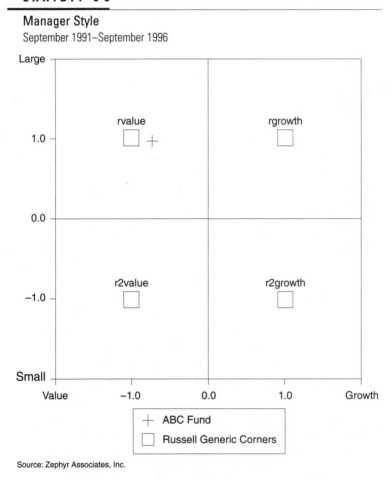

Source: Zephyr Associates, Inc.

5. William F. Sharpe, "Asset Allocation: Management Style and Performance
   Measurement," *The Journal of Portfolio Management,* Winter 1992, pp. 7–19.

quadratic optimization, one can determine a particular manager's precise correlation to each of the four pure "corners," in essence, his or her latitude and longitude on the style map. The small cross plots the manager's position relative to the map . . . his or her precise style point.

To understand how this works, imagine a world in which there were only two stocks: Growth and Value. Suppose you knew that Growth had a return of 20 percent last year and Value had a return of only 10 percent. If you knew nothing about Manager X except that his return was 10 percent last year, you'd know exactly which stock he held and hence his style at that point in time.

Benefits

There are several benefits to returns-based style analysis:

1. It is much easier and therefore cheaper than multifactor portfolio analysis. Formerly only the largest funds could justify the expense of such an analysis. Now, new software makes style analysis accessible, even to small funds.

2. If you can precisely pinpoint a manager's style, you can discover how much of his or her return is explained by his or her style. If the *unexplained* component is consistently positive, you can infer that you have discovered a skillful manager.

Exhibit 8–4 shows the value added for a particular manager versus his or her true benchmark (the dotted line) and also versus the S&P 500. At this point you might ask, "Since past performance in general has little predictive value, why should we assume that winners within a style might repeat, going forward?" Roger Ibbotson, a professor at the Yale School of Management, has conducted research which indicates that, in fact, performance within a style *does* have predictive value! He analyzed 1,007 mutual funds with at least 36 months of performance history. First, he developed

E X H I B I T 8–4

Performance/Cumulative Excess Return
Out-of-Sample Analysis

Source: Zephyr Associates, Inc.

a customized style benchmark for each fund using returns-based analysis. He then ranked winners within a style over one- and two-year periods. Next he compared the manager's "attribution" returns (manager's actual return – [prior period's exposure weights × the benchmark returns]). Managers who scored above the median were classified as winners; those below the median were called losers.

Ibbotson found that winners over a one-year period repeated the next year for 55 percent of the funds. Two-year winners repeated 54 percent during the next two years.

Most winners repeated in 13 of 14 one-year periods and in all 7 two-year periods. He found the results to be statistically significant.[6] This is meaningful! The implication is that through the use of returns-based style analysis, one can identify managers who *will be* skillful within a style.

The above study takes on great meaning in a multistyle portfolio, since if you have managers with multiple styles *and* rebalance the portfolio periodically, you are likely to have higher returns than the weighted average of the returns of each style. This effect occurs because you are forced to sell some of the winning manager's holdings (sell high) and redistribute the proceeds to the out-of-favor manager (buy low). When the favored style switches, as it inevitably will, you have proportionally more with the style which is *about to win* and less with the style which is about to lose.

Furthermore, you will not have to suffer through the prolonged periods of underperformance which plague funds managed under a single style. And you'll avoid the temptation to switch managers just before the favored style switches again.

3. Returns-based style analysis allows you to easily calculate a "completeness fund." A completeness fund counteracts style imbalance in your portfolio. By investing a portion of your fund in such a manner you will avoid inadvertent style bets (see Exhibit 8–5).

In this graph, the circle represents the current style of your portfolio, and the filled diamond is the style point required for the completeness fund. The open diamond is the resulting new style position of the overall portfolio.

4. Returns-based analysis also lends itself to historical analysis. You can easily note style "drift" over time. Exhibit

---

6. Roger G. Ibbotson, "Do Managers Repeat with Style?," *TMA Journal*, November/December 1996.

EXHIBIT 8–5

Manager Style
September 1996

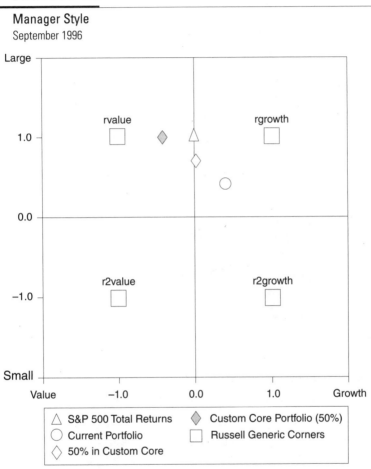

Source: Zephyr Associates, Inc.

8–6 shows a manager whose style has changed over time. The smaller crosses are earlier style positions; the larger crosses are more recent. You can see that this particular manager has gone from large growth to small value to small growth.

EXHIBIT 8–6

Manager Style
September 1991–September 1996

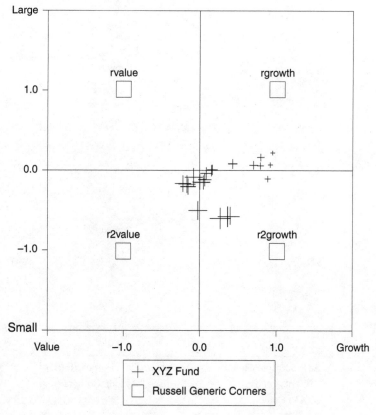

+ XYZ Fund
☐ Russell Generic Corners

Source: Zephyr Associates, Inc.

Style drift is problematic for several reasons: First, it will sabotage your efforts to maintain a style-neutral, multi-manager portfolio. Secondly, if the manager is "chasing" the style which is currently in vogue, he or she is likely to miss key turning points.

5. Returns-based style analysis can also help detect leverage or the use of derivative securities. Exhibit 8–7 shows a fund whose performance was so extremely growth oriented that it was unusual. We decided to allow the software to plot data which indicated short positions. The default setting

EXHIBIT 8–7

Manager Style
September 1991–September 1996

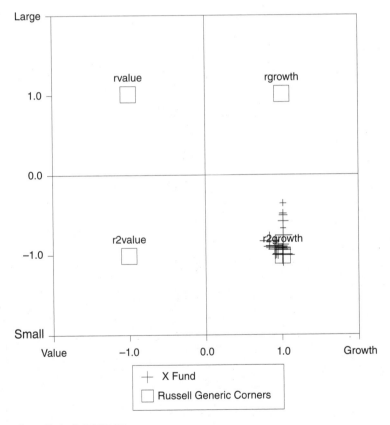

Source: Zephyr Associates, Inc.

allows long positions only. Exhibit 8–8 shows the results. The crosses are plotted beyond the +1 (100 percent growth position), indicating the use of leverage or derivative securities. A call to the portfolio manager elicited the comment, "We do allow the *conservative* use of options and futures" [italics ours]. This looks like a fairly high degree of leverage to us. Leverage helps in rising markets but causes larger losses during market declines, e.g., the margin calls in the crash of 1929. This fund has enjoyed significant outperformance during the recent bull market, but it seems as if there may be more downside risk than an investor might expect.

EXHIBIT 8–8

Manager Style
September 1991–September 1996

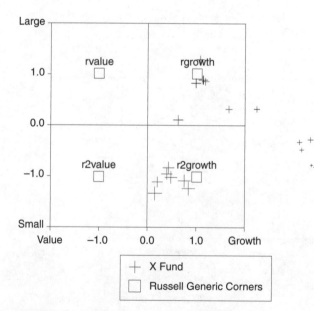

DRAWBACKS

As with any tool, there are certain drawbacks to this sort of methodology. In fact, returns-based style analysis seems to have generated a fair amount of criticism (although, to be fair, many of the critics sell competing services to retirement plans, endowments, and foundations). Some of negatives include:

1. Returns-based analysis doesn't reveal what *securities* are held within a portfolio; it only tells you how the portfolio behaved. For example, if you analyze a utility fund, it likely has performed as if the portfolio had a large component of bonds. Utilities are often purchased for their dividend yield. They also have a fairly large amount of outstanding debt as part of their capital structure. Therefore, the stocks tend to be very interest rate sensitive. A critic might say, "This analysis is inaccurate; there are no bonds in the portfolio."

The response might be, "Who cares! All I want is to understand how the portfolio acts." The flaw in that line of reasoning is that while the portfolio may have acted as if it contained bonds *in the past,* it may behave differently in the future. For example, one can imagine a scenario in which extreme energy inflation makes electric-powered vehicles cost-effective. In that environment, rising interest rates might not have a negative effect on electric utility stocks, although they surely would on bonds.

In other words, count on returns-based style analysis as an addition not a replacement for your other forms of analysis.

2. A potentially more serious flaw deals with the sophistication of your consultant or whoever utilizes the tool. Such software will *always* find a "best fit." In other words, if you regress the returns of your international manager against a style map consisting of only U.S. indices (large growth, large value, small growth, & small value), guess what? The software will plot a style point which best fits the data. Exhibit 8–9 shows an international index analyzed in this way. If you or your consultant do not have an inkling as to the manager's investment arena, you need to pay a great deal of attention to the performance attribution (R^2) of the

EXHIBIT 8-9

Manager Style
November 1989–September 1996

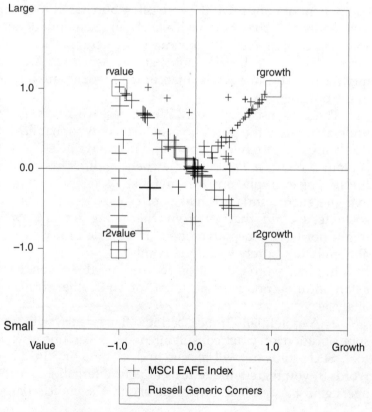

Source: Zephyr Associates, Inc.

analysis. A high R^2 (above 60 or 70 percent) indicates that there is a *good* fit; a low R^2 indicates that the fit is poor and, therefore, the style basis might be wrong. In Exhibit 8–10, the left-hand pie chart shows that the style benchmark has an R^2 of 15.7 percent (the benchmark explains only 15.7 percent of the performance for the above international analysis). Obviously this style basis is a poor fit.

   3. Another potential problem is that any type of style analysis will tend to push you away from managers whose style changes over time. If your fund is so small that you cannot implement a multistyle approach, a "sector-rotator" or other single manager whose style changes may be just the ticket.

   4. Returns-based analysis is quick and easy; however, it doesn't preclude the need for fundamental analysis. The risk is in assuming that the tool gives you all you need to know. In any case, the regressions never explain 100 percent of a manager's performance (an R^2 of 1); you have to dig to determine if the unexplained portion is attributable to skill, luck, or something else.

EXHIBIT 8–10

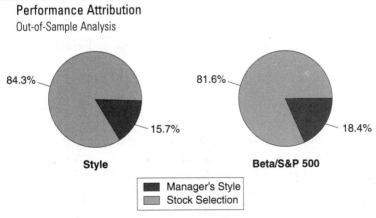

Performance Attribution
Out-of-Sample Analysis

84.3%

81.6%

15.7%

18.4%

Style

Beta/S&P 500

- Manager's Style
- Stock Selection

Source: Zephyr Associates, Inc.

THE NEW SOFTWARE

Several vendors currently supply software which will perform returns-based style analysis. Exhibit 8–11 provides a partial list of sources.

EXHIBIT 8–11

Software Sources

BARRA Associates	Zephyr Associates
1995 Universe Avenue	PO Box 12368
Berkeley, CA 94704	Zephyr Cove, NV 89448
Tel: (510) 548–4374	Tel: (800) STYLE-AD
Ibbotson Associates	Frontier Analytics, Inc.
223 N. Michigan Avenue	8910 University Center Lane
Suite 700	Suite 700
Chicago, IL 60601	San Diego, CA 92122
Tel: (312) 616-1620	Tel: (619) 552-1268
The Mobius Group	
68 T. W. Alexander Drive	
Research Triangle Park, NC 27709	
Tel: (800) 662-4878	

Source: DiMeo Schneider & Associates, L.L.C.

PRAGMATIC USES

To reiterate, style analysis should certainly be used in:

1. *Ongoing performance evaluation* (review Exhibits 8–5 through 8–9).
2. *Portfolio rebalancing* (review Exhibit 8–6).
3. *Special situations* (review Exhibits 8–8 and 8–9).
4. *Manager or fund searches.* In addition to the examples we've already discussed, there is a methodology which can be very helpful in the search process. Assume that you are hunting for a large-cap growth manager. Rather than beginning your search with

various qualitative screens such as manager tenure, assets under management, etc., as we describe in Chapter 10, you might first scan your database of managers, regressing each manager's returns against the style indices. You would then have an R^2 value for each fund against the large value, small value, large growth, and small growth indices (see Exhibit 8–12). Some of the available software will allow you to sort the funds by relative growth/value. You might first select all funds with coordinates 1.00 to 0.33 (the most growth-oriented third of the universe) and eliminate the rest. Note column labeled Value-Growth in Exhibit 8–13. You could then re-rank the survivors, according to size (1.00 to 0.33) and eliminate all but the largest third. Note column labeled Small-Large in Exhibit 8–14. By further sorting and eliminating managers on the basis of risk and return, you could quickly come up with a fairly tight list of candidates for more detailed fundamental analysis as described in Chapters 9 and 10.

SUMMARY

Style analysis can be a welcome and broad addition to your "toolkit." Recent research suggests that performance relative to a style category has predictive value. Furthermore, the analysis can help you understand the source of past performance and even point toward potential problems, such as excessive leverage or style drift. However, you need to remember that this tool does not replace the other, more traditional, forms of due diligence necessary for the prudent oversight of your fund.

In the next two chapters, we will explore the steps in an effective manager search.

EXHIBIT 8–12

Scan Analysis

Description	r2growth	r2value	rgrowth	rvalue	SB3MTB
AIM Constellation A	0.8538	0.00	0.1462	0.00	0.00
Brandywine	0.7097	0.00	0.2903	0.00	0.00
Crabbe Huson Special	0.1898	0.6188	0.00	0.0506	0.1409
Dreyfus Appreciation	0.00	0.1498	0.7256	0.00	0.1247
Evergreen Value Y	0.00	0.00	0.3073	0.5549	0.1377
Founders Discovery	0.8851	0.00	0.1149	0.00	0.00
Gabelli Value	0.25	0.16	0.00	0.3841	0.2059
Heartland Value	0.1634	0.7774	0.0125	0.00	0.0467
Invesco Emerging Growth	0.9933	0.0067	0.00	0.00	0.00
Janus	0.2339	0.00	0.4625	0.1237	0.18
Keystone Fund for Total Return A	0.00	0.00	0.2527	0.5112	0.2361
Lazard Small Cap	0.2885	0.7066	0.00	0.0049	0.00
MFS Value A	0.2765	0.1335	0.2924	0.2976	0.00
Neuberger & Berman Genesis	0.182	0.6703	0.0941	0.00	0.0536
Oppenheimer Target A	0.3391	0.2779	0.3829	0.00	0.0
Putnam Fund for Growth & Income B	0.00	0.0403	0.1891	0.6565	0.1141
Royce Premier	0.1189	0.2422	0.1411	0.0404	0.4575
Seligman Frontier A	0.8013	0.00	0.1987	0.00	0.00
Twentieth Century Giftrust Investors	0.9662	0.00	0.0338	0.00	0.00
USAA Growth	0.1355	0.00	0.6645	0.1132	0.0868
Van Kampen Amer Cap Emerging Growth B	0.8574	0.00	0.0076	0.135	0.00
Washington Mutual Investors	0.00	0.00	0.1418	0.7794	0.0788
Yacktman	0.00	0.00	0.7646	0.00	0.2354
Zweig Series Appreciation A	0.1617	0.3039	0.00	0.1862	0.3481

Source: Zephyr Associates, Inc.

E X H I B I T   8–13

Fund Ranking

Description	r2growth	r2value	rgrowth	rvalue	SB3MTB	Value-Growth
Seligman Frontier A	0.8013	0.00	0.1987	0.00	0.00	1.00
Twentieth Century Giftrust Investors	0.9662	0.00	0.0338	0.00	0.00	1.00
Founders Discovery	0.8851	0.00	0.1149	0.00	0.00	1.00
Brandywine	0.7097	0.00	0.2903	0.00	0.00	1.00
AIM Constellation A	0.8538	0.00	0.1462	0.00	0.00	1.00
Invesco Emerging Growth	0.9933	0.0067	0.00	0.00	0.00	0.9867
Yacktman	0.00	0.00	0.7646	0.00	0.2354	0.7646
Van Kampen Amer Cap Emerging Growth B	0.8574	0.00	0.0076	0.135	0.00	0.73
USAA Growth	0.1355	0.00	0.6645	0.1132	0.0868	0.6868
Dreyfus Appreciation	0.00	0.1498	0.7256	0.00	0.1247	0.5758
Janus	0.2339	0.00	0.4625	0.1237	0.18	0.5727
Oppenheimer Target A	0.3391	0.2779	0.3829	0.00	0.00	0.4441
MFS Value A	0.2765	0.1335	0.2924	0.2976	0.00	0.1377
Royce Premier	0.1189	0.2422	0.1411	0.0404	0.4575	–0.0227
Evergreen Value Y	0.00	0.00	0.3073	0.5549	0.1377	–0.2476
Keystone Fund for Total Return A	0.00	0.00	0.2527	0.5112	0.2361	–0.2586
Gabelli Value	0.25	0.16	0.00	0.3841	0.2059	–0.2941
Zweig Series Appreciation A	0.1617	0.3039	0.00	0.1862	0.3481	–0.3284
Neuberger & Berman Genesis	0.182	0.6703	0.0941	0.00	0.0536	–0.3942
Lazard Small Cap	0.2885	0.7066	0.00	0.0049	0.00	–0.423
Crabbe Huson Special	0.1898	0.6188	0.00	0.0506	0.1409	–0.4796
Putnam Fund for Growth & Income B	0.00	0.0403	0.1891	0.6565	0.1141	–0.5077
Heartland Value	0.1634	0.7774	0.0125	0.00	0.0467	–0.6016
Washington Mutual Investors	0.00	0.00	0.1418	0.7794	0.0788	–0.6376

Source: Zephyr Associates, Inc.

EXHIBIT 8-14

Fund Ranking

Description	r2growth	r2value	rgrowth	rvalue	SB3MTB	Value-Growth	Small-Large
Washington Mutual Investors	0.00	0.00	0.1418	0.7794	0.0788	-0.6376	0.9212
Evergreen Value Y	0.00	0.00	0.3073	0.5549	0.1377	-0.2476	0.8623
Putnam Fund for Growth & Income B	0.00	0.0403	0.1891	0.6565	0.1141	-0.5077	0.8053
Yacktman	0.00	0.00	0.7646	0.00	0.2354	0.7646	0.7646
Keystone Fund for Total Return A	0.00	0.00	0.2527	0.5112	0.2361	-0.2586	0.7639
USAA Growth	0.1355	0.00	0.6645	0.1132	0.0868	0.6868	0.6421
Dreyfus Appreciation	0.00	0.1498	0.7256	0.00	0.1247	0.5758	0.5758
Janus	0.2339	0.00	0.4625	0.1237	0.18	0.5727	0.3523
MFS Value A	0.2765	0.1335	0.2924	0.2976	0.00	0.1377	0.18
Gabelli Value	0.25	0.16	0.00	0.3841	0.2059	-0.2941	-0.0259
Royce Premier	0.1189	0.2422	0.1411	0.0404	0.4575	-0.0227	-0.1796
Oppenheimer Target A	0.3391	0.2779	0.3829	0.00	0.00	0.4441	-0.2342
Zweig Series Appreciation A	0.1617	0.3039	0.00	0.1862	0.3481	-0.3284	-0.2795
Brandywine	0.7097	0.00	0.2903	0.00	0.00	1.00	-0.4193
Seligman Frontier A	0.8013	0.00	0.1987	0.00	0.00	1.00	-0.6027
AIM Constellation A	0.8538	0.00	0.1462	0.00	0.00	1.00	-0.7075
Van Kampen Amer Cap Emerging Growth B	0.8574	0.00	0.0076	0.135	0.00	0.73	-0.7147
Crabbe Huson Special	0.1898	0.6188	0.00	0.0506	0.1409	-0.4796	-0.758
Neuberger & Berman Genesis	0.182	0.6703	0.0941	0.00	0.0536	-0.3942	-0.7582
Founders Discovery	0.8851	0.00	0.1149	0.00	0.00	1.00	-0.7703
Heartland Value	0.1634	0.7774	0.0125	0.00	0.0467	-0.6016	-0.9284
Twentieth Century Giftrust Investors	0.9662	0.00	0.0338	0.00	0.00	1.00	-0.9324
Lazard Small Cap	0.2885	0.7066	0.00	0.0049	0.00	-0.423	-0.9901
Invesco Emerging Growth	0.9933	0.0067	0.00	0.00	0.00	0.9867	-1.00

Source: Zephyr Associates, Inc.

9

CHAPTER

Manager Search

"When someone tells you of great past performance, work very hard to determine if it's likely to continue."

A Smart Consultant

"When a money manager tells you of the great things he will do tomorrow, ask him what he did yesterday."

Benjamin Franklin

In this chapter, we address an area that trustees and many investors enjoy most . . . the selection of specific managers or funds (by the way, unless otherwise noted, we will interchangeably use the terms "manager" and "fund"). This is one of the most important decisions you face. We'll outline a practical approach. In Chapter 10, we'll take an in-depth look at the selection process.

We previously asked you to think of your spending and investment policies as a "blueprint" for your fund. Now that the blueprint is drafted, it's finally time to start searching for the appropriate "contractors" (managers and funds).

Unfortunately, many endowments and foundations have done a poor job of selecting managers. With all good intentions, trustees often hire the local bank or investment advisor. While a show of support for the community is a noble idea, too often the manager is simply not qualified or appropriate for the fund. There are two primary reasons why you should be prudent and thorough in the selection process.

> **Reason #1:** *It's your fiduciary responsibility.*
> Manager selection requires prudence. You need sound reasons for your decisions. At some point you may have to demonstrate that your selection process was reasonable and thorough. Fiduciary standards keep ratcheting upward (see Chapter 12).

> **Reason #2:** *Enormous sums of money are at stake.*
> Earlier chapters correctly identified the asset allocation decision as the chief determinant of investment success at the portfolio level. However, the manager's results can still make or break your fund. Exhibit 9–1 illustrates the dramatic impact of an additional 1 percent annual return.

IT'S NOT AS EASY AS YOU THINK

Today the pure number of investment choices you face is staggering. Over 21,000 investment managers are registered with the Securities and Exchange Commission. This number has increased four-fold in the past 10 years! There are more mutual funds than stocks listed on the New York Stock Exchange. And virtually every business magazine or newspaper provides some sort of investment advice.

EXHIBIT 9–1

$10 Million Investment Value in 20 Years

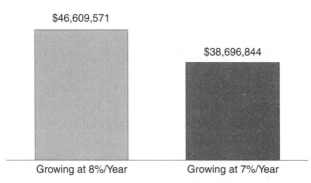

$46,609,571

$38,696,844

Growing at 8%/Year   Growing at 7%/Year

Source: DiMeo Schneider & Associates, L.L.C.

However, relying on general publications or word of mouth frequently leads to lousy results. The 28-year-old journalism major who picked the "10 Best" may have great writing abilities but only superficial financial knowledge. And assuming that the manager of your friend's endowment is "probably as good as anyone else" can be a real mistake. . . so can trying to take the easy way out by relying on popular fund or manager rankings.

Your fund has unique needs and objectives that should have been incorporated into your policy. A carpenter who builds an adequate garage isn't necessarily qualified to craft fine furniture. Apply this same logic to manager selection.

As we said, trustees who rely on the "top picks" of various non-professional publications can be in for a real surprise. Although more and more information has become available to all investors, it is important to understand the limitations. For example, a trustee may insist on choosing funds which are ranked highest by his or her favorite business periodical. This trustee doesn't understand that these "recommendations" are generic and don't address the endowment's specific policies in any way. Perhaps more importantly, published rankings are typically style-ignorant.

Ignoring manager style is a very serious mistake. See Chapter 8 for additional details. As we pointed out, there are two broad categories of stock-picking style. *Growth* managers try to identify companies with above average earnings growth rates. *Value* managers attempt to buy a dollar's worth of company for 50 cents. Both styles work, but they work at different times. In other words, the styles go in and out of favor. Style is the *prime* determinant of a manager's performance.

Unfortunately, most mass market publications ignore style. For example, *The Wall Street Journal* provides a great deal of useful mutual fund information each day. Investors can easily look up a fund's performance over various time periods and also obtain information on commissions and expenses. The *Journal* obtains this data from Lipper Analytical Services, Inc., one of the largest and most respected sources of fund information.

While much of the information is useful, the fund rankings can be confusing, if not misleading. The rankings compare performance among funds with the "same objectives." An **A** equals the top 20 percent for that period, a **B** equals the next 20 percent, and so on. The problem is that the objectives used to create the peer groups are frequently meaningless.

Lipper and the *Journal* group funds by investment category, such as "Capital Appreciation" or "Growth & Income." This process ignores investment style as well as market capitalization . . . *the two greatest determinants of return!* Exhibit 9–2 shows two funds, both with an investment objective identified as "Growth."

These two funds invest very differently; yet, they are compared to one another in performance rankings. This rating system gives real meaning to the disclaimer "past performance is not indicative of future results."

EXHIBIT 9–2

Prospectus Objective = Growth

Description

AARP Capital Growth - Seeks long-term growth. The fund invests primarily in undervalued common stocks and convertibles.... The fund is designed in cooperation with the American Association of Retired Persons (AARP) to meet the needs of persons over age 50.

Janus Enterprise - Seeks growth of capital. The fund invests primarily in common stocks of companies with market capitalizations of between $1 billion and $5 billion.... The fund may invest in special situations from time to time.... It may invest without limit in foreign securities.... The fund is nondiversified.

Comparisons

	AARP Capital Growth	Janus Enterprise
Median Market Capitalization	$12.3 Billion	$845 Million
Price/Earnings Ratio*	20.3	44.7
Investment Style	Value	Growth
Turnover Ratio	98%	194%

*Portfolio Average
Source: Morningstar, Inc.

IT'S NOT IN THE STARS

Morningstar, Inc. is another well-respected provider of financial information. Morningstar provides an extremely comprehensive financial analysis which includes risk, return, style, expense, and portfolio data. It also ranks funds according to a highly recognized star system. Ratings incorporate return and risk measures, and funds receive from one to five stars, with five being the best.

The problem is that investors often seek the easy answer and simply choose funds with five-star ratings. They don't understand how the funds are ranked and the inherent limitations of the process. To its credit, Morningstar regularly notifies investors that the star system is based on historical performance and should be just one of many tools used to select funds. Nevertheless, funds trumpet the star rating system in advertisements and reinforce the idea that the stars are all you need.

There are several reasons to dig deeper. For one, a fund's sales commission is incorporated into the ratings. For example, if a fund charges a 5 percent front-end commission, that amount is deducted from performance. What's the problem? Many funds that charge a sales commission at the retail level waive that commission for institutional investors such as endowments and foundations. Be aware that many funds would have received higher star ratings if commissions were not considered.

You also need to appreciate and understand which historical performance data is included and, perhaps more importantly, *excluded* in a star rating. Morningstar considers the most recent *complete* 3-, 5-, and 10-year periods. This means that a fund which began operations four years ago and bombed in its first year, but has had excellent performance since, may receive a four- or five-star rating. This focus on shorter-term performance may provide a distorted view. An investor who doesn't look beyond the stars can seriously misperceive the risk of the fund.

Another problem is that the rating systems ignore personnel changes. If the star stock picker who generated those five-year results just left the fund, what possible meaning can the rating have?

We are not knocking Morningstar or Lipper . . . just the opposite. We feel both services provide a great deal of useful information which can help investors. But the operative word is *help*. No rating system can replace the considerable amount of research and due diligence that should be performed . . . especially when the decision makers are held to fiduciary standards!

THE THREE-SWING APPROACH

We've made you aware of some of the pitfalls of the selection process; now we'd like to outline a prudent and hopefully profitable approach. We call our process the "three-swing approach" because we screen and review funds in three distinct phases.

The First Swing

We call the first swing the "prudent swing." It incorporates a number of *minimum* requirements which should be met in order for a fund to receive further consideration. If you look at Exhibit 9–3, you'll see that the first swing is not performance driven. An investment committee should agree on qualitative standards which must be met before performance

EXHIBIT 9–3

Minimum Criteria

- Greater than or equal to $500 million under management
- Median equity market capitalization of over $6 billion
- Foreign stock less than 15%
- Consistent asset allocations (stocks/bonds/cash)
- Manager tenure greater than or equal to 3 years
- Expense ratio less than 1.40% (group average)
- Consistent style emphasis
- Clearly defined investment process
- Organization: stability of personnel/infrastructure

Source: DiMeo Schneider & Associates, L.L.C.

is even reviewed. After all, what good is a historical track record if the investments don't mesh with your policy?

The Second Swing

You may be thinking: "It's fine to be practical and prudent, but you still need performance." You're right. After all, the assets must grow. So, a second and separate swing is performance analysis. But again we caution you: don't be awed by hot five-year returns; you have to dig much deeper.

You need to analyze performance in several ways. Exhibit 9–4 shows a variety of comparisons: absolute three- and five-year returns, standard deviation (a measure of volatility), the Sharpe ratio (a measure of risk-adjusted return), best and worst quarters, and quarter-by-quarter performance.

If you look at results from so many viewpoints, you'll better understand the complexities of past performance and judge its likelihood to continue.

We've taken two swings. Now it's time to compare the results of each.

The Third Swing

Ideally, the two lists will share some common names. If so, wonderful. You can perform additional analysis (manager interviews, on-site visits, etc.—see Chapter 10) to determine your finalists. If not, you may have to "relax" some of your original criteria (the beginning of your third swing).

As an example, a fund may have originally been bumped because of inadequate portfolio manager tenure. However, you see that same fund ranks very well on the performance screens. After additional analysis, you discover that the manager missed your tenure screen by only four months. As a result, you elect to include the fund for

EXHIBIT 9-4

Large Cap

	S&P 500		Fund 1		Fund 2		Fund 3		Fund 4		Current Fund	
3Q	5.35		13.36		4.01		6.25		3.28		5.28	
4Q 1991	8.38	NA	9.64	NA	3.32	NA	5.30	NA	3.92	NA	8.36	NA
1Q	(2.52)		2.51		1.13		(0.50)		3.48		(2.58)	
2Q	1.90		(2.95)		1.62		4.48		3.94		1.86	
3Q	3.15		4.76		1.65		2.79		2.60		3.08	
4Q 1992	5.03	7.61	11.68	16.39	6.10	10.84	5.28	12.50	3.40	14.11	5.00	7.40
1Q	4.37		5.59		7.82		5.47		6.15		4.34	
2Q	0.49		3.95		4.84		0.94		1.59		0.44	
3Q	2.58		7.24		3.40		4.27		3.28		2.54	
4Q 1993	2.32	10.08	0.85	18.71	1.28	18.38	2.01	13.24	3.10	14.83	2.29	9.92
1Q	(3.79)		1.44		(0.67)		(3.49)		(2.79)		(3.84)	
2Q	0.42		(4.20)		0.67		1.46		1.94		0.39	
3Q	4.89		7.21		5.43		6.11		5.54		4.86	
4Q 1994	(0.02)	1.32	(0.87)	3.28	(0.25)	5.16	0.03	3.93	(0.05)	4.53	(0.04)	1.19
1Q	9.74		9.52		9.68		8.27		8.13		9.70	
2Q	9.55		12.23		8.55		7.30		6.71		9.48	
3Q	7.95		11.36		7.99		6.95		7.42		7.94	
4Q 1995	6.02	37.59	(1.46)	34.88	3.76	33.40	6.00	31.70	7.60	33.37	6.01	37.43
1Q	5.37		0.52		6.30		5.48		4.94		5.36	
2Q	4.49	10.10	4.71	5.25	3.26	9.77	0.87	6.40	3.00	8.09	4.44	10.04
MAX Qtr	9.74		13.36		9.68		8.27		8.13		9.70	
MIN Qtr	(3.79)		(4.20)		(0.67)		(3.49)		(2.79)		(3.84)	
5-Year Statistics												
Return	15.73		20.28		16.77		15.73		16.21		15.56	
Std Dev	7.43		10.67		6.07		6.18		5.32		7.44	
R-Square	1.00		0.63		0.80		0.90		0.81		1.00	
Beta	1.00		0.90		0.65		0.75		0.58		1.00	
Sharpe	1.53		1.49		2.04		1.83		2.22		1.50	
3-Year Statistics												
Return	17.23		16.61		17.27		15.71		17.07		17.08	
Std Dev	8.10		10.84		7.02		7.13		6.64		8.10	
R-Square	1.00		0.68		0.95		0.93		0.95		1.00	
Beta	1.00		0.90		0.82		0.82		0.78		1.00	
Sharpe	1.71		1.22		1.98		1.73		2.06		1.69	

Source: DiMeo Schneider & Associates, L.L.C.

115

additional consideration. Although you've deviated from your initial criteria, it was a conscious decision. The third swing lends itself to a good helping of common sense.

This chapter introduced the manager search process and cautioned you against some of the pitfalls. The next chapter will show the finer points of an effective search.

10

The Search

In the last chapter we introduced the manager search process and examined potential pitfalls. In this chapter, we will take you through the process, step by step. We'll present specific screens which can help you choose a separate account manager (private manager) or mutual fund.

GETTING STARTED

Assume that you're on the investment committee of a mid-size endowment fund. Further assume that you have already taken the most important step and developed an appropriate asset allocation strategy. The allocation takes into account the committee's tolerance for risk and your current spending policy. Several asset classes are represented. The committee has decided to retain the current large-cap growth manager. Therefore, knowing the importance of maintaining a neutral overall investment style, you need to add a large-company U.S. stock fund that is *value* oriented.

In this example, we are searching for a fund as opposed to a manager; nevertheless, the process is virtually identical.

One of the first steps is to solicit formal input from the trustees and other key decision makers. Trustees are generally well-connected; many of them know investment professionals. You're eventually going to be asked why so-and-so wasn't considered; why not be proactive and solicit input up front? That way your search won't get derailed near completion when the committee member (who almost never attends meetings) suddenly shows up and demands that his or her neighbor, who "is a pretty darn good money manager," receive full consideration. Exhibit 10–1 is an example of a form to gather such input.

The First Swing

Begin with as broad a universe of potential candidates as possible. As discussed in the previous chapter, we suggest a three-swing approach. We'll show you some of the practical or prudent screens incorporated in the first swing.

As of this writing, Morningstar, Inc. identified and tracked 1,508 large-company funds. Too many, of course, for the investment committee to consider; so where should we start? The following screens will narrow the field. We also explain the rationale behind each so that you understand the process and can devise screens appropriate to your search.

Median Market Capitalization of Over $9 Billion. Since you're hiring separate small-company managers, it doesn't make sense to consider funds that own a good deal of small or midsize companies (generally $5 billion and over is considered large cap).

Greater Than $500 Million Under Management. Sometimes size can be a detriment, but not in this category. With at least $500 million under management, a fund has economies of scale. Note: Unlike *this* category, small-company stock managers can run into trading problems when they manage huge sums of money.

EXHIBIT 10–1

Committee Member Questionnaire

I. Investment Categories - Research will be performed to produce appropriate candidates for each investment category with a check mark.

☑ Money Market Funds   ☑ Large Company U.S. Stocks
☑ Stable Value/GIC Funds   ☑ Small Company U.S. Stocks
☑ Bonds (Investment Grade)   __ Global Funds (U.S. & Foreign)
☑ Balanced Funds   ☑ International Funds (Foreign Only)
__ Asset Allocation Funds   ☑ Real Estate Funds
__ High-Yield Bonds

Please indicate any additional investment categories which you strongly feel should receive consideration: _____

_____

II. General Screens - Dozens of screens will be used in each category. The following applies to most searches:

- Portfolio manager tenure of at least 3 years
- Below average fund expenses
- Adequate infrastructure
- Organization's depth and resources
- Administrative compatibility
- Reasonable growth in asset base
- Well-defined investment process
- Consistency of style
- Appropriate average market capitalization
- Risk-adjusted return
- Absolute return
- Returns in up markets
- Returns in down markets

Please provide any other specific criteria you would like incorporated into the screening process: _____

_____

III. Specific Funds/ Investment Organizations - Please indicate specific funds or organizations which you strongly feel should receive consideration. (Please provide as much detail as possible.)

_____

_____

_____

_____

Completed by: _____

Source: DiMeo Schneider & Associates, L.L.C.

Foreign Stock Holdings Generally Less Than 15 Percent. Again, no reason to replicate your foreign manager's holdings.

Cash Holdings Generally Less Than 10 Percent. For the trustees to be able to control the asset allocation, the managers must remain nearly fully invested.

Manager Tenure Exceeds Three Years. To ensure that those responsible for the track record are still around.

Consistent Style Emphasis. Since we're seeking value-style managers, we want to search the appropriate universe.

Expense Ratio Below the Group Average. (This is one screen which you would not use in a private manager search.) Expense is subtracted from return and furthermore has good predictive value (i.e., high-expense funds usually remain that way).

By simply applying the seven screens outlined above, the universe of funds narrows from 1,508 to 26. Think about that! We've eliminated 1,482 funds and haven't yet touched on performance.

The Second Swing

Now go back to the initial large-company fund universe and apply performance screens. When analyzing performance, it is extremely important to consider both absolute and risk-adjusted returns. You also want to evaluate several periods of time, as shown in Exhibits 10–2, 10–3, and 10–4.

We've taken two separate swings at our potential candidate list. Now let's search for common names. Managers who rank highly in both lists should be good possibilities for additional consideration.

Performance by itself is a bad predictor. Yet investment committee members sometimes question all these qualitative screens when it's really performance that they are after.

Academic studies have shown that past performance alone is a poor predictor of future performance. In one such study, Edgar W. Barksdale and William L. Green looked at 144 institutional equity portfolios over rolling 10-year periods between January 1, 1975, and December 31, 1989. The two wondered how often portfolios that finished in the *top 20 percent* of the group over the first five years would even finish in the *top half* over the next five years. Their study revealed a random pattern: top quintile performers in the first five years were actually the *least likely* to finish in the top half over the next five years.

Note: performance can be a useful predictor if utilized in conjunction with other crucial components, particularly investment style. Some of the earlier academic studies ignored style as well as other important qualitative issues. New studies lend support to the notion that good past performance can lead to good future results *provided you compare like managers.*

EXHIBIT 10–2

Performance Screens

Absolute Performance
- 1, 3 and 5 year averages
- 3 and 5 year rolling periods
- Up market analysis
- Down market analysis

Risk Adjusted Performance
- Sharpe ratio
- Treynor ratio
- Alpha measure

Relative Performance
- Appropriate indices
- Peer groups

Risk Measures
- Standard deviation
- Beta
- Downside risk

Source: DiMeo Schneider & Associates, L.L.C.

E X H I B I T 10–3

Return vs. Risk
Five-Year Trailing Ending September 30, 1996

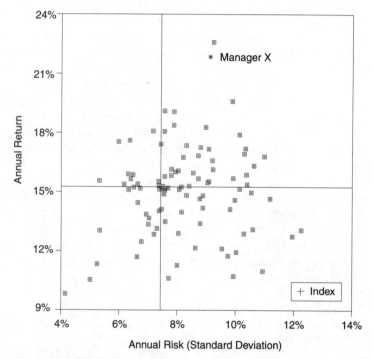

Universe: Mobius Group, Inc. Broad Large Cap.
Index: S&P 500 Index.

If five or more names appear on both lists, great! If not,
you may choose to relax one or more of the criteria in your
first swing. When relaxing screens, use common sense. For
example, it's probably okay to include a manager that has
$480 million under management, as opposed to your original
screen of $500 million. It's not appropriate to consider a fund
that routinely has one-third of its portfolio in foreign stocks.

The third swing involves additional fundamental
research on the remaining candidates. Conduct interviews
to gain insight into two key areas:

EXHIBIT 10–4

Manager X

Equity Funds - Segregated Accounts - Gross Equal (Equity Only)
Five-Year Trailing Ending September 30, 1996

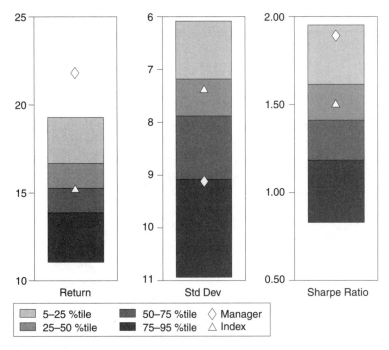

Universe: Mobius Group, Inc. Broad Large Cap.
Index: S&P 500 Index.

1. **The organization.** Discuss its infrastructure, stability of personnel, plans for dealing with growth, depth, and resources.

2. **The investment process.** Speak directly with portfolio managers and analysts (as opposed to a marketer) to judge whether the investment process is well defined and logical. Make sure that you receive a consistent story from different professionals at the same firm. Question their specific practices. How

does a security get on their buy list? Who decides, a person or a committee? When do they sell? What happens if they've made a mistake? Exhibit 10–5 is a short list of questions which can help.

E X H I B I T 10–5

Manager Due Diligence
Scope of Review

I. ORGANIZATION
  A. Financial Stability
  B. Infrastructure
  C. Qualifications and Stability of Personnel

II. INVESTMENT PROCESS
  A. Clearly Defined Manager Style/Investment Objectives
  B. Consistency of Style
  C. Portfolio Characteristics Appropriate with Style
  D. Adherence to Well-Defined Buy and Sell Disciplines
  E. Adequate Research Capabilities

III. PERFORMANCE
  A. Definition and Quality of Composites
  B. Consistency Among Accounts
  C. Client Performance in Line with Composite
  D. Reflective of/Consistent with Style

IV. OPERATIONS
  A. Adequate Systems
  B. Efficient Trading Operations
  C. Adequate Administrative Support
  D. Marketing/Client Servicing

V. COMPLIANCE/LEGAL
  A. Proper Registrations
  B. Code of Ethics, Supervisory/Compliance Manual
  C. Insurance Coverage
  D. ADV Current/Reflective of Services Rendered
  E. Proper Record Retention
  F. Soft Dollar/Directed Brokerage Practices

Source: DiMeo Schneider & Associates, L.L.C.

Once you have a short list, present meaningful information to the other committee members, not reams of data.
Exhibit 10–6 is an example of a presentation format that
may help them consider the candidates. If you've done a

E X H I B I T   10–6

Balanced Fund Analyses

Balanced Fund

The Screening Process

Three fund candidates are presented for review.

The search began with a database of 325 eligible funds. We initially applied
the following screens:

- Greater than or equal to $500 million under management
- Median equity market capitalization of over $6 billion
- Foreign stock less than 15%
- Consistent asset allocations (stocks/bonds/cash) year-to-year
- Manager tenure greater than or equal to 3 years
- Expense ratio less than 1.40% (group average)
- Consistent style emphasis
- Clearly defined investment process
- Organization: stability of personnel / infrastructure

Funds were ranked by risk, return, and risk adjusted returns and subsequent due diligence further narrowed the list of appropriate candidates.

Finalists

- Fund Company A Balanced
- Fund Company B Balanced
- Fund Company C Balanced

Fund Comparison Analysis

Balanced Fund

1. Fund Company A Balanced

The fund seeks capital preservation, current income, and long-term growth of
capital and income. It normally invests in a diversified array of equities, debt,
and cash instruments. These purchases may include common stocks, preferred
stocks, corporate bonds, or U.S. government securities. The equity portion

Exhibit 10–6, *continued*

includes foreign and domestic issues. Fixed-income securities must be rated investment-grade or above at the time of purchase. The fund primarily seeks issues that management believes demonstrate fundamental values at reasonable prices.

✔ Management team, since '75
✔ Med. Market Cap. $17.4 Billion/Value Style
✔ $3.5 Billion under management
✔ 54.3% Stocks, 32.6% Bonds, 11.9% Cash
✔ 86 stocks, 110 fixed income securities
✔ Expense ratio: 0.67%, 12b-1: 0.25%
✔ Average Maturity: 7.1 years
✔ Average Credit: AA, 1996 turnover rate: 39%
✔ Top five holdings: Phillips Petroleum, Wal-Mart Stores, 3M, Philip Morris, Treasury Note
✔ Conservative fund with only 1 losing year in the last 20

2. Fund Company B Balanced

The fund seeks income, conservation of principal, and long-term growth of principal and income. It may invest up to 75% of assets in common stocks and convertible securities. Prospective earnings and dividends are major considerations in these purchases. Individual securities are selected with regard to financial strength and economic background. The balance of the fund's assets are invested in investment-grade fixed income securities; unrated debt must be judged to be equivalent to those rated at least A. The fund may retain securities that have been downgraded below BBB.

✔ Management team, since '67
✔ Med. Market Cap. $9.1 Billion/Value Style
✔ $2.7 Billion under management
✔ 56.8% Stocks, 40.5% Bonds, 2.5% Cash
✔ 77 stocks, 75 fixed income securities
✔ Expense ratio: 0.57%, 12b-1: 0.0%
✔ Average Maturity: 11.6 years
✔ Average Credit: AA, 1996 turnover rate: 20%
✔ Top five holdings: Digital Equipment, General Motors, GNMA, Treasury Note, Dayton Hudson
✔ Inception date of fund June 1931

3. Fund Company C Balanced

The fund seeks capital appreciation and current income. It may invest in any type of security; ordinarily, no more than 75% of assets are invested in common stocks and convertibles. The balance may be invested in debt obligations

---

Exhibit 10–6, *concluded*

or money-market instruments. The debt portion may not contain securities rated lower than B. It may invest up to 20% of its assets in foreign securities.

✔ Management team, since '93
✔ Med. Market Cap. $11.4 Billion/Value Style
✔ $15.6 Billion under management
✔ 59.5% Stocks, 34.6% Bonds, 4.1% Cash
✔ 126 stocks, 233 fixed income securities
✔ Expense ratio: 0.91%, 12b-1: 0.25%
✔ Average Maturity: 11.5 years
✔ Average Credit: A, 1996 turnover rate: 103%
✔ Top five holdings: Treasury Note, Treasury Bond, Treasury Bond, GNMA, Treasury Bond
✔ Top five equity holdings: Weyerhaeuser, TRW, Philip Morris, Du Pont, General Motors
✔ The fund's equity component is run with a bias towards large company, value-oriented stocks

---

Source: DiMeo Schneider & Associates, L.L.C.

good job up to this point, any of the finalists should be well qualified to help you execute your strategy.

We suggest that the full committee consider qualitative issues first, just as you did in the selection process for finalists. Performance counts, but means a lot more if you understand what's "under the hood" of each fund. It's helpful if trustees have the information in Exhibit 10–6 as well as prospectuses, firm brochures, annual reports, and such well in advance of the selection meeting. Of course, most people will only read a portion of the materials, but for those who want it, the detail is there.

THE INTERVIEW

It is extremely important for the investment committee to interview the finalists. While each candidate should be able to do the job, one may be a better fit than others. You don't want to discover that half of the committee disagrees with the portfolio manager's philosophy *after* you've hired him or her. Yes, at this point it's a bit of a beauty contest, but you hope to make a decision you can live with for years. Why not pick the manager with whom you have the greatest rapport?

If you are searching for a private manager, it will be easy to arrange the interviews. Provided you meet account minimums, they will be glad to attend the presentation. If you're considering mutual funds or commingled trusts, it may be more difficult to get someone to present in person. However, you should arrange, at least, for a conference call.

Have the candidates present back-to-back. Also, give strict time limits and stick to them. For example, you might tell the managers to limit their presentation to 30 minutes with another 15 minutes for Q and A. Don't be afraid to tell a presenter, "You've got about 5 minutes left, do you have any final comments?" Be sensitive to the time commitment which your fellow committee members have made.

Make every effort to interview a *portfolio manager*. A slick marketer may be able to put a good spin on the presentation, but the actual decision maker can give you in-depth responses to your investment questions. Make certain that you ask all candidates the same questions. When it's time to make the final decision, there is nothing more frustrating than realizing that you forgot to ask one of the finalists a crucial question.

Isn't there an easier way? Why should the selection committee go though all this hassle? *Because it leads to better decisions!* If you thoroughly understand a manager or fund, you're more likely to understand the performance. You are less "wowed" by the numbers, and the selection process actually becomes simpler.

Armed with knowledge, the trustees will engage in open discussion and a sound decision should "bubble-up." Hint: If you have difficulty identifying the *best* fund among an outstanding group of finalists, it may be easier to reverse the process. Start looking for reasons, any at all, to eliminate funds. And remember, when all else is equal, expenses count.

OTHER IMPORTANT POINTS

The previous chapter communicated the importance of the manager search process and many of the pitfalls to avoid. So far in this chapter we have taken you through the steps involved in an actual search. In the balance of the chapter we'll present other important topics with which you should be familiar.

Sources of Information

As you can tell by now, analyzing managers or funds is a complex process. How can you even decide who should make the first cut? There are, of course, consulting firms which can help you tackle the chore (see Chapter 13). You can also purchase publications and other research tools in both written and electronic formats. (See Exhibit 10–7.)

Are These Returns Real?

A mutual fund is one large pool with many investors. Its performance is reported according to strict Securities and Exchange Commission guidelines. It's easy to obtain and verify fund results.

Not so with separate account managers. When these firms present performance, they use *composite figures*. A composite is only a mathematical calculation of the combined performance of a group of different accounts which the firm manages. The performance presented is a *synthetic* number.

There is nothing wrong with composite returns. In fact, how else could a separate account manager present performance? But you, as a fiduciary, must understand and feel comfortable with the construction of the composite. Be sure you or your consultant can answer these questions:

1. Which accounts are included in the composite?
2. Which are excluded?
3. Do the returns represent any *simulated* results?

EXHIBIT 10–7

Publications, Specialized Sources, and Software

Publications	Specialized Sources
The Wall Street Journal	*Morningstar, Inc.*
200 Burnett Road	225 W. Wacker Drive
Chicopee, MA 01021	Chicago, IL 60606
800-568-7625	800-876-5005
Investors Business Daily	*Valueline Mutual Fund Survey*
5959 S. Harlem	220 E. 42nd Street
Chicago, IL 60638	New York, NY 10017-5891
312-229-0402	800-833-0046
Barrons Magazine	*Pension & Investments*
1 S. Wacker Drive	965 E. Jefferson Avenue
Chicago, IL 60606	Detroit, MI 48207
312-750-4190	800-678-9595
Forbes Magazine	
60 5th Avenue	**Software**
New York, NY 10011	*Morningstar*
800-888-9896	see above
Fortune	*Mobius Group, Inc.*
Time Life Building-Rockefeller Plaza	68 T. W. Alexander Drive
New York, NY 10020	Research Triangle Park, NC 27709
800-621-8000	800-662-4878
Business Week	*Zephyr Associates Inc.*
1221 Avenue of the Americas	Post Office Box 12368
39th Floor	Zephyr Cove, NV 89448
New York, NY 10020	702-588-0654
800-635-1200	

Source: DiMeo Schneider & Associates, L.L.C.

4. Are accounts size-weighted or equally weighted?

5. Are returns gross or net-of-fees?

6. Do the composite results presented comply with standards established by either the Investment Management Consultants Association (IMCA) or the Association for Investment Management and Research (AIMR)?

The presentation standards identified in question six were created to help make composite results more meaningful. Both IMCA's version (the Consultants' Performance Standards) and AIMR's version (the Performance Presentation Standards) require managers to be uniform and consistent when presenting returns. The standards differ in the fact that IMCA does not require cash balances to be included with other segments (e.g., equity or fixed income). IMCA also requires an *unweighted* average of the composite accounts, while AIMR allows *weighted* averages. One large account has more impact on the composite figures than several small accounts.

Ideally, the managers will comply with either IMCA or AIMR performance standards, and their results will have been verified by an independent third party. Although more and more money management firms claim compliance, fewer than 10 percent have had performance verified. Ask if your candidate is among them.

Passive Versus Active Management

Since asset allocation is the key component of return, and manager or fund selection is so complex, why not just buy the index? After all, in some categories index funds routinely beat at least half the actively managed funds, and expenses tend to be dirt cheap.

In recent years, the popularity of index funds (funds that merely purchase all the securities of a particular index like the S&P 500) has grown tremendously. However, keep the following points in mind when you consider this option.

1. **To index is to strive for average.** If you think about it, the return of an index should, over time, equal the average return of all investors in a given market. While it's better to be average than below average, there is a huge universe of fund and manager candidates for trustees who seek to outperform the averages.

2. **Indexing works best in very efficient markets.** It is difficult for a portfolio manager to add value if his or her stock selections must be made exclusively from a list of very large U.S. companies ("blue-chips"). Blue-chip stocks are well researched and highly liquid. It's hard for a given manager to know anything special about those stocks that is not already widely understood (and, therefore, "in the stock price").

3. **Indexing makes the least sense in inefficient markets.** The markets for small-company stocks and non-U.S. stocks are *not* very efficient. Foreign stock managers must make many decisions involving countries, currencies, regional economies, and so on. Additionally, many foreign companies simply aren't well researched. All of this creates plenty of opportunity for smart money managers to add value.

4. **Indexing wins—sometimes.** Things go in cycles. If you analyze historical results, you'll see that passive investing (indexing) has soundly beaten active investing for several years. However, if you had looked at the same comparisons ending in 1994, you would have seen the opposite effect. A lot depends on your starting and ending points. Contrary to popular opinion, active managers have their day in the sun, as well. Index investing appears to be at a peak in popularity right now because we're in a cycle where the S&P 500 has outperformed most active managers, and, of course, the public loves a winner.

Trustees might want to hedge against these cycles by using both passive and active managers in their fund. Also, with indexing comes the *full* risk of the market. If your goal is to preserve capital in down markets, you may wish to seek active managers who have a record of performing well during down markets.

Managers Versus Funds

There is no absolute right or wrong. Generally, as an endowment fund increases in size it can access private managers (who typically have higher minimum investment requirements). The benefits of separate account management include portfolio customization and lower expenses. Also, private managers don't have to deal with the inopportune inflows and outflows of cash, which mutual funds face. Peter Lynch, for example, did a terrific job running Fidelity Magellan. He might have done even better if he didn't have to deal with investors' money pouring in at market highs and racing out at market lows.

On the other hand, mutual funds can be very appropriate investments, even for large endowments or foundations. Mutual funds provide easy access to niche areas such as foreign markets and real estate.

Fee Negotiations

It is generally easier to negotiate fees with private managers. Again, the funds are closely regulated and fees are specified in the prospectus. However, some funds have a special institutional class of shares, or their prospectus may allow certain expenses to be waived.

Regardless of whether you're hiring a manager or a fund, you should seek a "most favored nation" clause in your contract. That is, the manager acknowledges, in writing, that your fees will be at least as low as those of any similar endowment or foundation clients of your manager.

Also, find out whether special fee schedules apply to non-profit organizations; it never hurts to ask.

Administrative Compatibility

Although this is not usually a problem, be sure the managers or funds you're considering can be easily accessed. For example, some mutual funds or commingled trusts can only be purchased by retirement plans. Others may require you to use a particular custodian.

Trade Execution

With separate account managers, you must understand their policy on trading. Do they demand good commission rates? Perhaps more importantly, do they obtain good execution? Because commissions and trade executions directly impact the performance of your fund, you should be satisfied that the manager trades on a fair and equitable basis. How does the manager allocate trades? If trades are too large to be executed in one block, later trades usually receive worse prices than do earlier transactions. How are the favorable prices allocated?

Social Investing

Some endowments and foundations have policies that restrict the types of companies in which they may invest (e.g., no gambling or tobacco stocks). If your fund imposes restrictions, be sure to incorporate them into your screening process.

Traditionally, social investing meant that trustees identified restricted industries and found managers who would avoid purchases in those industries. Now, some money managers offer a more proactive approach. They actively seek out socially responsible companies for investment.

Proxy Voting

Corporations regularly ask their shareholders to vote on a variety of issues. This can be done in person at an annual meeting, or the shareholder can appoint a proxy to vote in his or her place. Trustees often delegate the responsibility of voting proxies to investment managers. If you choose to do this, be sure that your managers acknowledge their responsibility in writing and that they have procedures in place to vote on proxies and to document their actions. ERISA plans are required to document this, and it's a good idea for endowments and foundations as well.

KEY MANAGER EVALUATION STATISTICS

Numerous statistics and ratios are used to compare managers and funds. The definitions in Exhibit 10–8 should prove useful.

Manager Questionnaires

Questionnaires are used to gather a variety of information about managers. The questionnaire in Exhibit 10–9 was developed by IMCA. It is an outstanding tool that can help in the due-diligence process.

Now that you've selected managers to implement your investment policy, the job's over, right? . . . Wrong! Unfortunately, in the real world, things don't always work out. It's crucial that you maintain a close watch over the fund. In Chapter 11, we will explore the topic of ongoing performance evaluation.

EXHIBIT 10-8

Key Definitions

The Modern Portfolio Statistics presented here were computed by regressing quarterly returns of each respective manager/fund against the appropriate market index.

Standard Deviation
Risk can be stated as the standard deviation of returns around the mean or average return. Risk is a part of any financial investment decision and must be analyzed along with other facets of a potential investment. The level of return is directly related to the level of risk the investor experiences. Risk is also referred to as volatility. Typically, the higher the volatility of returns, the more likely the actual return from an investment will differ from the expected return. While positive volatility is welcome, negative is not.

R Squared "Coefficient of Determination"
A measure of diversification, R^2 indicates the extent to which fluctuations in portfolio returns are explained by market action. For a fund where $R^2 = 1.0$, all (100%) of its returns are market-determined, indicating a completely diversified portfolio balanced across all segments of the market. An $R^2 = 0.70$ implies that 70% of the fluctuation in a portfolio's return is explained by the fluctuation in the market. In this instance, overweighting or underweighting of industry groups or individual securities is responsible for 30% of the fund's risk.

Beta
A measure of risk, it indicates a fund's sensitivity to market changes. Funds with $\beta = 1.0$ are equal in volatility to the market, while funds with $\beta = 0.75$ are only 75% as volatile as the market. Accordingly, a fund with a 1.10 beta is expected to perform 10% better than the market in up markets and 10% worse in down markets. Because beta analyzes the market risk of a fund by showing how responsive the fund is to the market, its usefulness depends on the degree to which the markets determine the fund's total risk (indicated by R^2).

Sharpe Ratio
The ratio is essentially a fund's return divided by its standard deviation and provides a measure of portfolio efficiency. This ratio measures return per unit of total risk (or "risk-adjusted" return). Hence, the *higher* the Sharpe ratio, the more reward you are receiving per unit of total risk. This measure can be used to rank the performance of mutual funds or other portfolios.

Treynor Measure
A fund's return divided by its beta. This ratio also measures return per unit risk (or "risk-adjusted" return). The *higher* the Treynor ratio, the more reward you are receiving per unit of risk. The Sharpe and Treynor measures provide complementary but different information. This measure can be used to rank the performance of mutual funds or other portfolios.

Alpha
A measure of the nonsystematic return, it is the return that is not attributable to the market or the risk level of the investment. If the market's return was zero, then the manager's expected return would be alpha. The higher the alpha, the more *value* a manager is adding to the performance of a portfolio over the market.

Source: DiMeo Schneider & Associates, L.L.C.

EXHIBIT 10–9

IMCA Questionnaire

INVESTMENT MANAGEMENT CONSULTANTS ASSOCIATION

- STANDARDIZED METHODS OF MEASURING PERFORMANCE RESULTS

- STANDARDIZED INVESTMENT MANAGER QUESTIONNAIRE

Exhibit 10–9, *continued*

❖

Standardized Investment
Manager Questionnaire

❖

Please read the following instructions before completing this questionnaire:

1. All questions must be completed.
2. All answers must be typewritten or legibly printed.
3. If any questions are not applicable or the answer is not available,
   please answer as N/A.
4. If any answer is larger than the space available, please include in an
   attachment which references the page and section number. Answer only the
   question asked. Any additional information required will be requested.

This questionnaire is in compliance with the Consultant's Performance Standards.

Exhibit 10–9, *continued*

Investment Manager Questionnaire

I. BACKGROUND INFORMATION

   A. Firm Name & Address

      Firm Name: _____

      Address: _____

      City: _____ State: _____ Zip: _____

      Telephone: _____ Fax: _____

   B. Contacts

      Questionnaire completed by: _____ Title: _____

      Primary client contact: _____ Title: _____

      Backup client contact: _____ Title: _____

   C. Ownership & Affiliates

      Your firm is organized as a: _____

      List ALL owners of your firm: _____

      _____

      Explain owners' relationship to firm: _____

      _____

      List ALL related companies: _____

      _____

      Explain related companies' relationship to firm: _____

      _____

      _____

   D. Other offices

      List the locations where the firm has other offices: _____

      _____

Exhibit 10–9, *continued*

E. History

List names, positions held and dates of all professional-level personnel added in the last 5 years:

_____

_____

List names, positions held and dates of all professional-level personnel departures in the last 5 years:

_____

_____

Provide information pertaining to any organizational changes that have occurred over the past 10 years that a prudent investment professional would consider significant:

_____

_____

F. Important Dates

Date assets were first managed: _____/_____/_____

Date current investment process initiated: _____/_____/_____

Date present firm was operative: _____/_____/_____

Exact date of SEC filing _____/_____/_____   SEC file # _____

G. Personnel

1. Total employees: _____

   Portfolio Managers :   _____

   Analysts (NOT included above):   _____

   Client Service/Marketing (NOT included above):   _____

   Administrators (NOT included above);   _____

   Other Professionals (NOT included above):   _____

   Traders (NOT included above):   _____

   Other full-time employees (NOT included above):   _____

2. Provide an organizational flow chart.

2

Exhibit 10–9, *continued*

3. Indicate the number of portfolio managers and analyst specialists for equity, fixed income and other assets:

	Equity	Fixed Income	Other Assets
Portfolio Managers	_____	_____	_____
Analysts	_____	_____	_____

H. Indicate the name of your insurance carrier and the dollar amount:

Errors & Omissions _____ $ _____

Fiduciary Liability _____ $ _____

II. ASSETS AND BREAKDOWN

A. Assets managed and number of portfolios.

	Employee Benefit Plans (tax exempt) Discretionary	Non-Discretionary
Corporate:	$ _____ / _____	$ _____ / _____
Taft-Hartley:	$ _____ / _____	$ _____ / _____
Public:	$ _____ / _____	$ _____ / _____
Other: _____ (describe)	$ _____ / _____	$ _____ / _____
Total (1):	$ _____ / _____	$ _____ / _____

	Other Tax Exempt	
Endowment/Foundation	$ _____ / _____	$ _____ / _____
Insurance:	$ _____ / _____	$ _____ / _____
Other: _____ (describe)	$ _____ / _____	$ _____ / _____
Total (2):	$ _____ / _____	$ _____ / _____
Total Tax Exempt (1 & 2)	$ _____ / _____	$ _____ / _____
Total Taxable:	$ _____ / _____	$ _____ / _____
Total Collective Trusts/ Mutual Funds	$ _____ / _____	$ _____ / _____

3

Exhibit 10–9, *continued*

B. Largest, median, and smallest discretionary accounts currently being managed.

	Tax Exempt	Taxable
Largest	_____	_____
Median	_____	_____
Smallest	_____	_____

C. Assets managed and numbers of portfolios by asset size.

Balanced Assets

Size	Market Value	# of Portfolios
Under $1MM	_____	_____
$1MM - $10MM	_____	_____
$10MM - $25MM	_____	_____
$25MM - $50MM	_____	_____
$50MM - $100MM	_____	_____
Over $100MM	_____	_____
Totals	_____	_____

Equity

Size	Market Value	# of Portfolios
Under $1MM	_____	_____
$1MM - $10MM	_____	_____
$10MM - $25MM	_____	_____
$25MM - $50MM	_____	_____
$50MM - $100MM	_____	_____
Over $100MM	_____	_____
Totals	_____	_____

4

143

Exhibit 10–9, *continued*

Fixed Income

Size	Market Value	# of Portfolios
Under $1MM		
$1MM - $10MM		
$10MM - $25MM		
$25MM - $50MM		
$50MM - $100MM		
Over $100MM		
Totals		

Other Assets

Size	Market Value	# of Portfolios
Under $1MM		
$1MM - $10MM		
$10MM - $25MM		
$25MM - $50MM		
$50MM - $100MM		
Over $100MM		
Totals		

Describe other assets: _____

_____

_____

_____

_____

_____

_____

Exhibit 10–9, *continued*

D. List the market value at time of addition and the number of accounts gained in each of the last 5 calendar years:

	Market Value	# of Portfolios
19 ____	$ _____	_____
19 ____	$ _____	_____
19 ____	$ _____	_____
19 ____	$ _____	_____
19 ____	$ _____	_____

E. List the market value at time of departure and the number of accounts lost in each of the last 5 calendar years:

	Market Value	# of Portfolios
19 ____	$ _____	_____
19 ____	$ _____	_____
19 ____	$ _____	_____
19 ____	$ _____	_____
19 ____	$ _____	_____

F. Explanation of account departures and additions.

_____

_____

_____

_____

_____

_____

_____

6

Exhibit 10–9, *continued*

III. INVESTMENT PROCESS

A. Describe your firm's overall investment philosophy for both equity and fixed income securities.

Exhibit 10–9, *continued*

B. Methodology

Indicate all styles which describe your equity management.

	Most Applicable	Partially Applicable	Not Applicable
Top-Down			
Bottom-Up			
Value Oriented			
Defensive/High Yield			
Contrarian			
Theme Selection			
Sector Rotation			
Growth			
Emerging Growth			
Tactical Asset Allocation			
Market Timing			
Quantitative			
Large Capitalization			
Medium Capitalization			
Small Capitalization			
Core Equity			
Hedged Equity			
Socially Responsible			
Non-Diversified			
Other*			

Indicate all styles which describe your fixed income management.

	Most Applicable	Partially Applicable	Not Applicable
Passive			
Active			
Maturity Ladder (Buy-Hold)			
Immunization			
Credit Analysis			
Duration			
Interest Rate Anticipation			
Sector Swapping			
Maturity Swapping			
Other*			

* Explain: _____

_____

_____

8

Exhibit 10–9, *continued*

C. Investment Strategy

Within your investment process, rank the order of importance (1 being highest):

Asset Mix   (   )   Diversification/Concentration   (   )

Sector/Industry   (   )   Other (explain in addendum page)   (   )

Individual Security   (   )

List the relative importance of each of the following decisions (each column should add to 100%)

	Asset Mix	Sector/Industry	Security	Diversification/ Concentration	Other
Single Decision Maker	_____%	_____ %	_____%	_____ %	_____ %
Portfolio Manager					
Invsmt Policy Committee					
Research					
Other (explain below)					
Totals	100	100	100	100	100

D. Asset Allocation

List the end of quarter asset allocation percentages for the past 5 calendar years, for equity, balanced, fixed income and any other accounts.

		Equity Eq./Cash	Balanced Eq./Fixed/Cash	Fixed Fixed/Cash	Other (Describe) /Cash
19____	1Q	/	/ /	/	/
	2Q	/	/ /	/	/
	3Q	/	/ /	/	/
	4Q	/	/ /	/	/
19____	1Q	/	/ /	/	/
	2Q	/	/ /	/	/
	3Q	/	/ /	/	/
	4Q	/	/ /	/	/
19____	1Q	/	/ /	/	/
	2Q	/	/ /	/	/
	3Q	/	/ /	/	/
	4Q	/	/ /	/	/
19____	1Q	/	/ /	/	/
	2Q	/	/ /	/	/
	3Q	/	/ /	/	/
	4Q	/	/ /	/	

Exhibit 10–9, *continued*

		Equity Eq./Cash	Balanced Eq./Fixed /Cash		Fixed Fixed/Cash	Other (Describe) /Cash
19___	1Q	/	/	/	/	/
	2Q	/	/	/	/	/
	3Q	/	/	/	/	/
	4Q	/	/	/	/	/

E. Investment Decision Process

Describe the process by which an investment idea is originated and implemented. Include a flow chart.

_____

_____

Provide the names and titles for all members of the investment policy or strategy committee.

_____

_____

_____

_____

_____

What individual discretion does each portfolio manager have in structuring portfolios (   )%

What is the frequency of regularly scheduled investment policy or strategy meetings:_____

Exhibit 10–9, *continued*

F. Research

Provide name and title of the most senior employee charged with your research activities:

Name: _____ Title: _____

What is the frequency of regularly scheduled research meetings:_____

What is the approximate number of securities generally followed: _____

What is the average number of securities on your "buy" list: _____

and what is the maximum number: _____

Indicate how you measure risk (i.e., Standard Deviation, Beta, Quality) in choosing individual securities and structuring portfolios: _____

_____

_____

What percentage of the investment process is based on technical analysis: (0 to 100%):

Overall Market   (   )%   Individual Securities   (   )%

List your ten largest equity positions as of the end of the last 5 calendar years (no symbols) and the % allocation to a typical portfolio.

	19____	19____	19____
1			
2			
3			
4			
5			
6			
7			
8			
9			
10			

11

Exhibit 10–9, *continued*

	19___	19___
1		
2		
3		
4		
5		
6		
7		
8		
9		
10		

What percentage of the research effort comes from various sources (must add up to 100%)

Wall Street Research ( )%   Research Vendors (i.e., Value Line) ( )%

Regional Brokerage Research ( )%   Internal Original Research ( )%

Annual Reports 10K, etc. ( )%   Other (explain in addendum) ( )%

Company Visits ( )%

What percentage of your brokerage transactions are allocated to purchase research _____%.

G. Disciplines

Describe any "sell discipline" or "watch list" designed to realize profits and cut losses, reduce risk, or provide quality control. Explain when such a discipline will be enacted:

_____

_____

_____

_____

_____

Indicate the average number _____, the largest number _____, and the smallest number _____ of issues in a fully invested equity account.

Exhibit 10–9, *continued*

If a client does not provide you with objectives and guidelines, how do you establish guidelines?

_____

_____

Provide the average or typical portfolio characteristics for:

Dividend Yield _____ %   Price/Book Value _____   PE Multiple _____

Average Market Capitalization _____

Are your portfolios managed by one manager, separate equity and fixed managers, or by teams?

_____

What is the average number _____ and the maximum number _____ of portfolios managed by one portfolio manager?

Describe your policy regarding diversification:

_____

_____

_____

_____

Describe how you control portfolio risk:

_____

_____

_____

When you purchase a security, what is your time horizon?

_____

_____

_____

_____

13

Exhibit 10–9, *continued*

H. Trading

Provide the name and title of the most senior employee charged with your trading activities:

Name: _____ Title: _____

How many employees are involved with trading your portfolios: _____

How many broker-dealers have you regularly traded with over the last calendar year: _____

Describe any restrictions you may have on client directed transactions: _____

_____

_____

List the average annual turnover per account (the minimum of purchases and sales):

Equity _____% Balanced _____% Fixed _____% Other _____%

Complete in detail your policy regarding commission discounts for stocks and bonds:

Discount from current posted rates   (   )%   Bonds usually done @ $ /credit per bond

Discount from May 1, 1975 rates   (   )%   Option Contracts @ _____each

Trades usually done @ $_____/share   Other (explain in addendum)

I. Fees

Please list or attach your fee schedule.

What is the minimum tax-exempt account your firm will accept? _____

What is the minimum taxable account your firm will accept?_____

What is the minimum annual fee? _____

Under what circumstances are your fees negotiable? _____

_____

What is your billing frequency? _____

If you have a different fee schedule for eleemosynary or public fund clients, attach and label them.

Exhibit 10–9, *continued*

IV. CLIENT SERVICES

A. Provide name and title of the most senior employee charged with client service:

Name: _____ Title: _____

B. How many employees are involved with client services? _____

C. Provide a breakdown for a portfolio manager's allocation of time (must add to 100%):

Client Contact	(	)%	Portfolio Management	(	)%
Administrative Duties	(	)%	Trading	(	)%
Investment Research	(	)%	Marketing (new business)	(	)%

D. Indicate the minimum frequency for various forms of communication for all clients:

Telephone Calls: _____ Periodic Portfolio Reviews: _____

Market Letters: _____ Individual Issue Reviews: _____

Attach samples of market letters, portfolio and individual issue reviews.

E. Describe your policy regarding client meetings at both the client's offices and your offices:

_____

_____

_____

V. BUSINESS PLANS

A. Indicate what your future plans may be involving both investment management or other business activities:

_____

_____

_____

_____

_____

_____

15

Exhibit 10–9, *continued*

B. Indicate the details of any new investment services you plan to introduce:

_____

_____

_____

_____

_____

_____

_____

C. Do you have any plans to cap or limit your growth in terms of total assets $ _____, and total number of portfolios _____?

Describe: _____

_____

_____

D. What emphasis are you placing in the following areas regarding future business (must add to 100%)?

Corporate:	( )%	IRA & 401K:	( )%
Public Funds:	( )%	Taxable:	( )%
Taft-Hartley:	( )%	Other:	( )%

Describe "Other": _____

_____

E. Describe any past or pending regulatory action or litigation. Please attach formal filings.

_____

_____

_____

16

Exhibit 10–9, *continued*

VI. PERFORMANCE DATA

NOTE: It is imperative that Section VII - PERFORMANCE DATA STANDARDS be read and fully understood BEFORE providing the information required in this section. Failure to read and understand Section VII may result in improper data for this section.

The following 5 methods of measuring and presenting performance are ranked here in their order of preference and desirability; 1 is most desirable and 5 is least desirable. Indicate in the appropriate location which of the 5 methods applies for each composite presented.

1. The composite results presented comply fully with the Consultants Performance Standards, and have been verified by an independent third party (proof of verification should be attached).

2. The composite results presented comply fully with the Consultants Performance Standards, but have not been verified by an independent third party.

3. The composite results presented comply fully with the Consultants Performance Standards for the time periods presented, but full retroactive compliance has not been undertaken.

4. The composite results presented partially comply with the Consultants Performance Standards, and an explanation of the non-compliance items has been clearly presented.

5. The composite results presented do not comply at all with the Consultants Performance Standards, and an explanation of the exact nature of their construction has been clearly presented.

17

Exhibit 10–9, *continued*

NOTE: If clearly presented computer generated performance results are available, they may be attached to this questionnaire in lieu of completing the specific sections listed below. Be sure, however, to fill in below or clearly indicate on the computer generated forms the qualitative items listed below.

A. Composite Performance Results (Make as many copies of this page as needed to present each composite's result., i.e., multiple composites, gross and net returns for the same composite, unweighted and weighted returns for the same composite, etc.)

   1. General investment category (equity, fixed income, other):_____

   2. Specific composite description (investment style): _____

   3. Indicate which of the above mentioned performance reporting methods applies (1-5):

   4. Composite returns are unweighted_____or weighted _____.

   5. Composite results are gross _____or net _____of investment management fees.

   6. If a segment composite (i.e., equity, fixed income), cash balances are _____are not _____ included in the underlying data.

   7. Check appropriate boxes: returns are calculated on a trade date_____, settlement date_____, accrual basis_____, cash basis_____.

   8. Rates of returns presented represent live results _____or simulated results _____.

   9. Calendar quarter and annual rates of returns

	1st Quarter	2nd Quarter	3rd Quarter	4th Quarter	Full Year
19___					
19___					
19___					
19___					
19___					
19___					
19___					
19___					
19___					
19___					
19___					

   10. Is this composite shown in conformance with the AIMR standards?_____

18

Exhibit 10-9, *continued*

NOTE: If clearly presented computer generated composite statistics are available, they may be attached to this questionnaire in lieu of completing the specific sections listed below.

B. Additional Information

1. For as many quarter ends as possible, present the following minimal information regarding each composite. Where quarterly information is not available, annual information should be presented as a minimum.

   a. The number of accounts included in the composite.

   b. The number of accounts with a similar investment style.

   c. The total number of accounts under management.

   d. The total market value of included accounts.

   e. The average unweighted size of the accounts in the composite.

   f. The average weighted size of the accounts in the composite.

   g. The largest account in the composite.

   h. The median account in the composite.

   i. The smallest account in the composite.

   j. The average asset allocation of the composite (equity, fixed income, cash & equivalents, other).

   k. The highest individual account rate of return in the composite.

   l. The median individual account rate of return in the composite.

   m. The lowest individual account rate of return in the composite.

   n. The standard deviation of individual account returns about the composite average on a quarterly or annual basis.

   o. The average PE for the composite, where appropriate.

   p. The average yield for the composite, where appropriate.

   q. The average market capitalization for the composite, where appropriate.

   r. The average maturity for the composite, where appropriate.

   s. The average quality rating for the composite, where appropriate (indicate which rating service).

19

Exhibit 10–9, *continued*

2. Calendar quarter and annual composite statistics

Item #	1st Quarter	2nd Quarter	3rd Quarter	4th Quarter	Full Year
a.					
b.					
c.					
d.					
e.					
f.					
g.					
h.					
i.					
j.					
k.					
l.					
m.					
n.					
o.					
p.					
q.					
r.					
s.					

3. Composite Disclosure Information

   a.   Provide appropriate disclosure information as required by the Consultant's Performance Standards and the AIMR Performance Presentation Standards.

20

Exhibit 10–9, *continued*

VII. PERFORMANCE DATA STANDARDS

NOTE: The following information is extracted from the Consultant's Performance Standards, Section 2 - I. Consult the full standards document for further explanation. Also note that the Consultant's Performance Standards differ from the AIMR Performance Presentation Standards in several respects. (1) The cash balances are not required to be included with other segments (i.e., equity or fixed income) when calculating segmented performance; (2) Composite results should be an unweighted average of the component accounts .

A. Type of Data

1. The investment manager should provide information on as many separate performance composites as necessary to ensure that the consultant's needs are properly represented by a product offered by the investment manager. Every fully discretionary account under management should be included in its style composite.

2. For certain types of investment managers, (for example, bank trust departments, mutual fund organizations, and insurance companies), investments are frequently managed using commingled funds. When creating style composites, these commingled funds should be treated just like an individual account.

3. Composite performance data should be presented on a gross (before fee) basis, as permitted by the SEC in "one-on-one" presentations. Wherever possible, composite performance data should be presented on a net (after fee) basis also.

    a. Fees should be handled in compliance with the SEC rules regulating the advertising of investment performance. Adequate information should be provided so that the consultant's client can be presented with returns on both a gross and net basis.

    b. A current copy of the manager's fee schedule should be presented in conjunction with the investment manager's results.

4. Cash balances for the individual accounts constituting a composite should be handled in a manner consistent with the investment management of the account where practically possible.

    a. If cash is considered to be a separate asset class, then any cash and related assets should be segregated as a distinct asset class.

    b. Any cash considered for investment purposes to be part of another asset class (such as equities) should be included with the other asset class where practically possible.

    c. Isolating cash as a separate asset class will enable the consultant to properly analyze various aspects of the investment management process such as security selection and market timing.

Exhibit 10–9, *continued*

B. Time Periods

1. The preferred rate of return data is either monthly or calendar quarter time weighted rates of return for each relevant inception of the firm, inception of the relevant investment style, or the latest 10 years, whichever period is shorter. Rate of return data for periods longer than 10 years is certainly acceptable but not required. Returns for cumulative periods are desired, but not necessary if quarterly information has been supplied since they can be calculated.

C. Return Calculations

1. A time-weighted total rate of return calculation that minimizes the impact of contributions and withdrawals is mandatory.

2. The preferred method for calculation of fund quarterly rates of return is to link monthly returns.

   a. The preferred frequency of data for calculation of monthly returns is monthly market values and daily cash flows.

   b. As a minimum, the quarterly return could be calculated using quarterly market values and monthly cash flows

3. When a cash flow in excess of 10% of a portfolio or segment occurs, and the interim market value is available or can be obtained, interim time-weighted calculations should be performed for that month.

4. The preferred method of calculating fund returns is on a trade date and accrual basis. Whenever this is not possible, settlement date and cash basis accounting may be used. Income should not be calculated on an estimated or pro-rated basis.

D. Composites

1. Each composite should include all fully discretionary client accounts of a similar style, both past and present, for whatever time period such accounts are under management. Inclusion should begin with the account's first full performance measurement period, either monthly or quarterly, and end with its last full measurement period, either monthly or quarterly. Accounts should not be included in a composite for only portions of the period during which the account is under management.

2. Composite performance should be calculated by equally weighting the performance of the individual accounts. Composite returns weighted by account size may also be presented if desired.

3. Balanced fund composites should include only those accounts over which the investment manager has full discretion with respect to asset allocation.

22

Exhibit 10–9, *continued*

4. The segmented portions (such as equity or fixed income) of balanced accounts may be included in their respective segment composites (such as an equity only composite) only if the investment manager maintains separate accounting for those segments of a balanced account, thereby allowing the performance of the asset classes to be separated. The various segmented portions of the individual accounts contained in the segment composite need to be treated consistently regarding any associated cash balances.

5. An account using leverage should be included in the appropriate composite only if its performance is calculated on a non-leveraged (full-cash) basis.

6. Information on any exclusions from or changes in a composite being presented should be shown.

7. Composite performance data should not be altered to reflect personnel or other organizational changes. Any significant internal changes within the firm should be properly disclosed.

8. The creation of a composite should not be arbitrary. The investment style represented by the composite must be capable of being replicated, and the investment process must be logical and prudent.

9. The performance of any client accounts which are no longer under management should always remain in the historical composite performance data.

E. **Simulated Results**

1. The investment manager may use simulated performance results if actual results do not exist for a defined investment process and the simulated results have been requested by the consultant.

2. Simulated returns should never be linked with actual results to provide an analysis of long term investment performance unless specifically requested by the consultant.

3. It is encouraged that actual results be calculated along side of the simulated results to facilitate analysis of the investment strategy being used.

4. Out of period sampling of simulated results is the preferred methodology, that is, the investment process represented by a particular set of simulated results should also be implemented during a separate time period outside the time range of the simulated results.

F. **Transferability of Historical Record**

1. Any past investment results belong to the investment management firm which achieved those results, not any single individual.

2. The manager may present performance results achieved by key investment personnel while employed with another investment advisory organization if those professionals are implementing that same investment process at the new management firm. However, that data must not be linked with results achieved at the new firm, and disclosure of these circumstances to the consultant is crucial. Listed below are several cases where transference of the past investment record makes sense:

   a. If continuity of clients exists, and the track record can be traced back for those clients, then transferability should be allowed.

Exhibit 10–9, *concluded*

b. If an investment firm is sold, but the investment personnel remain consistent with the same investment philosophy, then transferability should be allowed.

3. Any use of past investment results from a prior investment management firm will be scrutinized closely.

a. Any differences between the current firm structure and the prior firm structure will be analyzed and disclosed.

b. These differences might include changes in the investment committee, the support staff, the internal/external research capability, or the firm size.

c. Particular attention will be given to past returns resulting from a "committee" process being attributed to only several members of that committee.

4. Returns representing prior firm performance and current firm performance should not be linked. The two sets of returns should be presented separately for their corresponding time periods.

5. Any significant changes in personnel or structure which may affect future performance should be disclosed.

24

Source: Investment Management Consultants Association (IMCA)
9101 E. Kenyon Avenue, Suite 3000
Denver, Colorado 80237
303/770-3377.

11
CHAPTER

Evaluate Performance

Once you have completed your search and managers are in place, you must begin an ongoing evaluation process. Remember the old adage, "the best laid plans . . ." The perfect game plan cannot guarantee future results. You must keep a fair and constant eye on manager performance to ensure that you meet your goals and objectives. Before you run out and purchase monitoring software or contract for evaluation services, ask yourself this basic question: "What do we want from our portfolio and each manager?" There are a number of possibilities.

The simplistic answer is "the highest return possible." That may be an appropriate objective for an aggressive small-cap manager, but it is, without doubt, the wrong objective for a core fixed income manager. You need to be more thoughtful and specific. Maybe you want the manager to achieve a set rate of return, to stay ahead of inflation by a certain percentage, to beat the market, or to surpass the performance of his or her peers. Perhaps you want the manager to meet all of these goals. Perhaps you have specific risk parameters. Different evaluation methods naturally arise from these different performance objectives. Like a master carpenter, you need to select the right tools. Your ruler will be the appropriate benchmarks.

Fortunately, the investment industry can supply you with the resources you require. Of course, you'll rely on some of the same tools you used in the manager selection process. Again, recent research points out the key role of manager style. Given the strong correlation of style (growth or value, large-cap or small-cap, etc.) to performance, style-based analysis must be part of your evaluation tool kit.

BENCHMARKS

You may want to start with two straightforward, fundamental benchmarks: a *nominal* return objective and an *inflation-adjusted* rate of return. These measures are the basic building blocks in a performance monitoring program. State your desired, or nominal, rate of return as a simple, static target percentage, for example, 10 percent. An inflation-adjusted goal is merely the return you require above the inflation rate. The current consumer price index can serve as a proxy for inflation. For example, your fund might require a return of the CPI + 5 percent.

While these benchmarks are a starting point, such simple comparisons are insufficient to evaluate a large fund with a varied asset allocation. Additional style-specific benchmarks provide a more individualized and fruitful evaluation process. Your benchmarks will typically include both market indices and universes of peer groups. Use both types, because they fulfill different needs.

Market Indices

A market index is the rate of return on a hypothetical portfolio. The index tells you that if you had invested in *these* securities for *this* period, you would have gotten *this* return. (With the emergence of index funds, many indices are also real portfolios—see Chapter 10.)

The available indices are numerous and varied. An index can be *broad-based*, that is, comprised of a large number of securities and designed to indicate the movement of the whole market. It can also be *narrow-based*, containing a smaller number of securities and designed to represent the price movement of a particular market sector. Narrow-based indices attempt to avoid overlap with other sectors. They may also exhibit characteristics of a particular style.

An index can employ a variety of weighting strategies. In order to calculate a return, each component of an index must be assigned a relative weight. For example, in a *cap-weighted index*, the rate of return of each stock is weighted in proportion to the market capitalization of that stock. Some indices simply assign *equal weights* to each component security, regardless of capitalization or price. The emergence of returns-based style analysis adds yet another point of differentiation. Imagine the permutations: A broad-based industrials index; a large-company value, cap-weighted index; a small-cap growth, equal-weighted index; and on and on.

Multiply the number of options by the number of financial companies which supply indices. For example, the S&P 500, produced by Standard & Poor's Corporation, is a cap-weighted, broad-based index comprised of 400 industrial stocks, 40 financial stocks, 40 utility stocks, and 20 transportation stocks. The companies in the index have large market capitalizations. If you take just the 400 industrial stocks, you've got the S&P Industrials. The S&P

MidCap 400 is comprised of another 400 stocks of smaller, mid-range capitalization, from the same market sectors represented in the 500 index.

The Frank Russell Company also produces equity market indices. It, too, divides the equity market by capitalization, but further subdivides the market into growth and value segments. For example, the Russell 1000 index is comprised of the 1000 largest companies listed on U.S. exchanges or traded in the over-the-counter markets. The Russell Value Index calculates the rate of return on the stocks in the Russell 1000 that exhibit "value" characteristics, such as a low price-to-earnings ratio, a low price-to-book ratio, and so on. The Russell Growth Index consists of the stocks in the Russell 1000 that have "growth" characteristics, above-average growth rates, high P/Es, and so on.

The fixed income market boasts its own family of indices. Lehman Brothers, Merrill Lynch, and Salomon Brothers all provide bond indices that slice and dice the bond market into specific sectors and styles. For example, the Lehman Brothers Government/Corporate Index is made up of fixed income securities that are: ranked in one of the top four grades by the various rating agencies; issued by the U.S. government or one of its agencies; and of various maturities including long-term (maturities longer than 10 years). The Lehman Intermediate Government/Corporate Index is similar in composition but is limited to an average intermediate maturity (maturity dates in the 5- to 10-year range).

Multiple Benchmarks

Although the selection of indices can be daunting, the variety available makes for sophisticated evaluation. Several indices can be used in the analysis of one fund; for example, an equity manager might be compared against the S&P 500, a bond manager against the Lehman Brothers Aggregate

Bond, and the fund composite against a combination of the two. The indices selected will be a prime component of your written investment policy.

Since they are so varied and numerous, you should take great care to select the index, or combination of indices, that most closely approximates your fund's objectives. Unfortunately, too many fiduciaries use the seat-of-the-pants method to select market benchmarks. There are better methods. One approach might be to compare the securities and weightings in your managers' portfolios to those which comprise various benchmarks. You could then select the benchmark(s) that seems to have the best fit. This approach would be fairly labor intensive, especially given the need to track the appropriateness of the index over time.

A better method might be to utilize the same type of returns-based analysis described in Chapter 8. By regressing the returns of your portfolio against various indices, you could identify the index with the highest statistical correlation and lowest tracking error compared to your portfolio.

Get Real

Be sure that your benchmarks are realistic estimations of market performance—that they are investable and measurable. A good benchmark can be thought of as an alternative to active management. For example, a benchmark of "the median large-cap manager" is an uninvestable standard. You would have no way of knowing what that portfolio might be until after the fact. Such a benchmark is reminiscent of Will Rogers's method for beating the market: "Buy stocks. Those that go up, you keep. Those that go down, you don't buy."

Once the benchmark is chosen, it is imperative that you apply the indices consistently for as long as the fund's objectives remain unchanged. We have seen many examples of selective benchmarking. That is, for one quarter managers compare their results to the S&P 500; the next quarter they benchmark themselves against a mid-cap growth index. The third quarter they compare themselves to "the average growth fund." Somehow the managers seem to compare favorably to the ever-changing benchmark . . . imagine that.

Exhibit 11-1 shows a comparison of a particular manager to the target "policy." *Policy* is the index which has been selected as the most appropriate comparison for this particular manager. In this example, the investment advisor is a large-cap equity manager; therefore, the policy is the S&P 500 Index. If the manager had run a balanced portfolio, the policy might have been a blend consisting of 60 percent S&P 500 Index and 40 percent Lehman Brothers Intermediate Government/Corporate Index.

E X H I B I T 11-1

Manager XYZ: Trailing Returns Through June 30, 1996

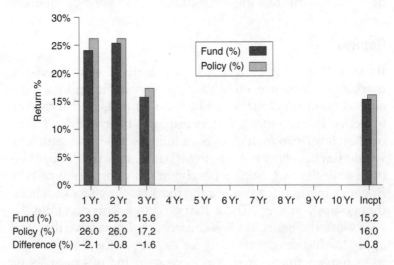

	1 Yr	2 Yr	3 Yr	4 Yr	5 Yr	6 Yr	7 Yr	8 Yr	9 Yr	10 Yr	Incpt
Fund (%)	23.9	25.2	15.6								15.2
Policy (%)	26.0	26.0	17.2								16.0
Difference (%)	−2.1	−0.8	−1.6								−0.8

Source: Mobius Group, Inc.

INTERPRETING THE DATA

In Exhibits 11–1 and 11–2 we see that Manager X has trailed the target policy for the past one-, two-, and three-year periods as well as in the current quarter. So, what do you do? Should you fire a manager because performance has fallen below that of the policy benchmark for a quarter or year? First of all, *every* manager will underperform his or her benchmark for some period. Secondly, it may be that the manager doesn't hit the cover off the ball in up markets but outperforms in down markets.

Exhibit 11–3 shows the same kind of comparison, but divides the period into up markets and down markets. An up market is defined as all the quarters within a period in which the policy had positive returns. In Exhibit 11–3 we

E X H I B I T   11–2

Manager XYZ: Calendar Returns

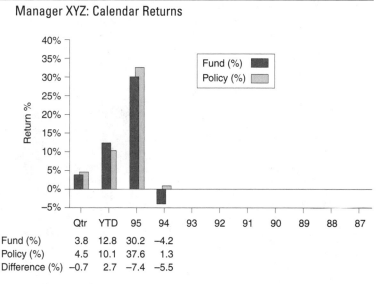

	Qtr	YTD	95	94
Fund (%)	3.8	12.8	30.2	−4.2
Policy (%)	4.5	10.1	37.6	1.3
Difference (%)	−0.7	2.7	−7.4	−5.5

Source: Mobius Group, Inc.

EXHIBIT 11–3

Manager XYZ: Up Market Returns and Down Market Returns

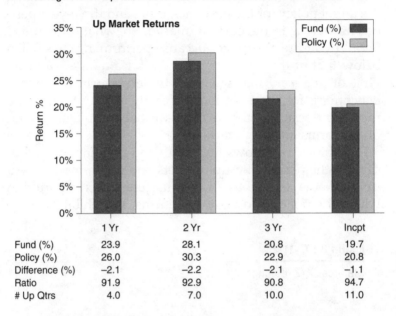

	1 Yr	2 Yr	3 Yr	Incpt
Fund (%)	23.9	28.1	20.8	19.7
Policy (%)	26.0	30.3	22.9	20.8
Difference (%)	−2.1	−2.2	−2.1	−1.1
Ratio	91.9	92.9	90.8	94.7
# Up Qtrs	4.0	7.0	10.0	11.0

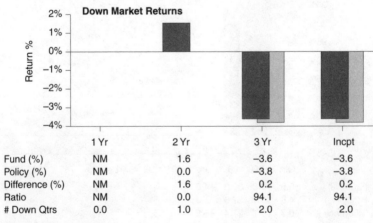

	1 Yr	2 Yr	3 Yr	Incpt
Fund (%)	NM	1.6	−3.6	−3.6
Policy (%)	NM	0.0	−3.8	−3.8
Difference (%)	NM	1.6	0.2	0.2
Ratio	NM	0.0	94.1	94.1
# Down Qtrs	0.0	1.0	2.0	2.0

Source: Mobius Group, Inc.

see that Manager X has not captured all of the upside but has lost much less than the average in the down periods. This may be exactly what you hired the manager to do.

Market indices are useful tools because they are widely recognized and easy to find. Their major shortcoming is that they do not specifically replicate an active manager's style. An active manager purports to beat the market, to go beyond merely mimicking a market index. Peer group analysis can provide a more specific means of comparison.

PEER GROUP UNIVERSE

While indices reflect the potential return in the market for any given period, peer group comparisons represent the "real world" returns actually achieved by active fund management. You can complement your benchmark evaluation by judging a manager against a universe of his or her peers. You can purchase universe data from organizations (like the Mobius Group or Wilshire Associates) that collect, maintain, and analyze data on a large number of investment managers. Many consultants maintain similar databases. In addition, consultants may belong to a cooperative which constructs performance universes. Each member of the co-op contributes its clients' performance numbers and thereby gains access to the common database of returns.

In order for a universe to be meaningful, it must be large and pure. You should judge a universe database on its size; the more entries or data-points, the better. You should also evaluate the construction of a universe. The factors used to populate a universe should be consistent with your style definitions and consistently applied throughout the database. Be wary of a database that manipulates logarithms in order to artificially beef up a particular style for which sufficient data doesn't exist.

Sub-universe Construction

Consulting firms increasingly rely upon style-specific "sub-universes" to get a clearer understanding of the performance of a particular manager. A sub-universe is a specific component of a broad universe (e.g., small-cap, growth stock managers). A leading vendor of universe data and performance evaluation software separates domestic equity managers into the sub-universes shown in Exhibit 11–4.

Access to tightly specified peer groups can enable you to get a true "apples to apples" comparison. Compare your pure small-cap aggressive growth equity manager's performance to a universe of other pure small-cap aggressive growth managers. Exhibit 11–5 shows a peer group universe comparison. The vertical axis designates the rate of return. The horizontal axis divides the graph into time periods: the quarter, year-to-date, 1995, and so on. There is a "floating bar chart" for each period representing the performance of the particular universe during that period. The performance data of a universe of broad, large-cap core managers is ranked and then divided into quartiles. For example, in Exhibit 11–5, the 1995 performance of the second quartile managers ranged from 31.0 to 35.4 percent.

Fund or manager performance is then plotted within the floating bar charts for easy, visual interpretation. The open diamond represents the performance of your manager. The open triangle represents the performance of the policy. Specific numbers are given in the text at the bottom. For each fund or manager and index, the rate of return is accompanied by its actual rank in the universe.

WHAT DOES IT MEAN?

Imagine it's January 1, 1995: Should you fire this manager because his or her performance placed him or her in the bottom quartile over the past year? Every manager, regardless of his or her skill level, will spend some time in the bottom

EXHIBIT 11–4

Universe Composition

	Universe Name	Weighting Criteria	Tracking Error Criteria	Index
	Broad Equity			
	Broad Large-Cap	≥ 50% Large-Cap	≤ 7.0	Russell 1000
	Pure Large-Cap	≥ 75% Large-Cap	≤ 7.0	Russell 1000
	Broad Large-Cap Value	≥ 50% Large-Cap Value	≤ 7.0	Russell 1000 Value
	Pure Large-Cap Value	≥ 50% Large-Cap Value	≤ 7.0	Russell 1000 Value
	Pure Large-Cap Growth	≥ 50% Large-Cap Growth	≤ 7.0	Russell 1000 Growth
	Pure Large-Cap Growth	≥ 75% Large-Cap Growth	≤ 7.0	Russell 1000 Growth
	Broad Small-Cap	≥ 50% Small-Cap	≤ 11.0	Russell 2000
	Pure Small-Cap	≥ 75% Small-Cap	≤ 11.0	Russell 2000
	Broad Small-Cap Value	≥ 50% Small-Cap Value	≤ 11.0	Russell 2000 Value
	Pure Small-Cap Value	≥ 75% Small-Cap Value	≤ 11.0	Russell 2000 Value
	Broad Small-Cap Growth	≥ 50% Small-Cap Growth	≤ 11.0	Russell 2000 Growth
	Pure Small-Cap Growth	≥ 75% Small-Cap Growth	≤ 11.0	Russell 2000 Growth

Source: Mobius Group, Inc.

EXHIBIT 11–5

Manager XYZ: Universe Comparisons
Broad Large Cap Core

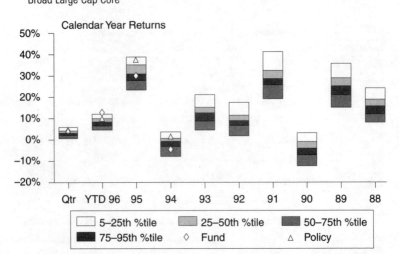

Calendar Year Returns

	Qtr	1996	1995	1994	1993	1992	1991	1990	1989	1988
Fund										
Return	3.8	12.8	30.2	–4.2						
%tile	32	1	55	80						
Policy										
Return	4.5	10.1	37.6	1.3						
%tile	19	20	9	18						
Universe										
5th %tile	5.8	12.0	39.1	3.8	21.1	17.5	41.5	3.1	35.8	24.4
25th %tile	4.2	9.9	35.4	0.7	15.1	11.6	32.6	–1.0	29.2	18.9
50th %tile	3.1	8.3	31.0	–0.8	12.5	8.7	28.9	–4.2	25.2	15.8
75th %tile	2.1	6.7	27.8	–3.2	8.9	6.7	25.8	–7.1	21.2	12.1
95th %tile	0.5	4.3	23.5	–7.9	4.4	1.8	19.2	–12.3	14.9	8.1

Returns are in percent. "%tile" is the percentile ranking within the universe.
Returns for periods exceeding one year are annualized.

Source: Mobius Group, Inc.

quartile. You need to determine: Is this merely one of those unfortunate aberrant events, or have the wheels fallen off?

First, you need to isolate the problem. You must keep in mind that the graph of 1994 consists of four cumulative periods and therefore gives cumulative performance numbers. Before the addition of the most recent one or two quarters, this manager's numbers may have looked fine. You can look at non-cumulative quarters to locate where performance began to lag. Analyze other, security-specific data (as discussed in the remainder of this chapter) for changes that coincide with periods of poor performance. In a typical scenario, the manager may have owned stocks in an out-of-favor industry, for example, cable television. While private cable transactions may have occurred at 10.5 times cash flow, stocks in the same industry may have sold off to the level of 5 times cash flow. In 1995 and 1996, the manager was eventually proven right. However, in 1994, those positions caused underperformance.

Talk to your manager. You want the problem to be both contained and explicable. Follow the manager closely over the next months. If poor performance continues, you may want to implement a change. But remember, return is only part of the evaluation. Risk must also be considered.

PORTFOLIO ANALYSIS

In addition to rates of return, many databases also maintain portfolio holdings. These identify each security and its value, or weight, in the portfolio. You can easily compile and weight individual security characteristics (such as industry sector, price/earnings, beta, etc.) to build an accurate picture of the characteristics of the portfolio as a whole. Security-specific analysis allows you to understand the extent to which the portfolio's characteristics affected performance. In short, portfolio analysis enables you to look beyond mere performance.

Attribution Analysis

Any investment committee wants to know if the fees it pays to an investment manager are justified. To determine whether or not a manager adds value, you need to pinpoint the source of return in a portfolio. A manager may perform well because the index that guides his or her investment decisions performs well, or because the industry he or she emphasizes performs well. Also, a manager may outperform an index or an industry by picking exceptional stocks within that index or industry. By accessing a database that analyzes the performance and characteristics of specific securities, you can separate the return achieved through asset allocation, sector and industry selection, weighting, and stock selection—a form of analysis called *performance attribution*. Put simply, this analysis attempts to differentiate skill from luck. The bottom line is that you want good stock-pickers. A manager skilled in individual stock selection will be more likely to consistently add value over time.

Exhibit 11–6 outlines how an individual portfolio's return compares to an index return, in this case the S&P 500, by isolating each industry and its weighting. In the first column you see the individual portfolio broken down: The weighting of each industry (A) and the rate of return on each industry (B). You can read a line in this column as "the stocks in consumer non-durables industry (which represents 20.2 percent of the portfolio) achieved a 6.3 percent rate of return." The second column illustrates the same two factors (C & D) for the S&P 500 portfolio. The numbers in the third column show the differences between the individual portfolio and the S&P 500 portfolio. A positive number in column E, "Stock," tells you that the manager added value

EXHIBIT 11–6

Performance Attribution, Manager C
Quarter Ending 6/96

	Portfolio		S&P 500		Selection		
	Pct. of Market Value A	Rate of Return B	Pct. of Market Value C	Rate of Return D	Stock E	Industry F	Total G
Consumer Non-Dur	20.2	6.3	23.5	7.8	−0.3	−0.1	−0.4
Consumer Durable	3.8	−0.9	3.5	−1.6	0.0	0.0	0.0
Basic Industry	9.9	−4.9	6.8	−4.2	−0.1	−0.3	−0.3
Capital Goods	14.0	−0.2	19.7	7.7	−1.1	−0.2	−1.3
Health Care	18.1	5.6	10.5	4.0	0.3	0.0	0.2
Energy	5.9	−0.7	8.9	4.5	−0.3	0.0	−0.3
Transportation	8.6	0.9	1.6	1.6	−0.1	−0.2	−0.3
Utilities	1.5	2.7	11.4	4.4	0.0	0.0	0.0
Finance	16.4	2.4	13.0	1.8	0.1	−0.1	0.0
Miscellaneous	1.6	1.3	1.1	1.2	0.0	0.0	0.0
	100.0%	2.2	100.0%	4.6	−1.5	−0.9	−2.4

Equity Only Return	1.6
Buy & Hold Return	2.2
Active Management Value Added	−0.6

Stock (E) $= A \times (B - D) / 100$
Industry (F) $= (A - C) \times (D - \text{Index Return}) / 100$
Selection (G) $= E + F$

Source: Canterbury Consulting Services.

by selecting stocks which outperformed the stocks in the S&P 500 $[E = A \times (B - D)/100]$; a positive number in column F, "Industry," means that the manager added value by weighting the particular industry more heavily than it is weighted in the S&P 500 $[F = (A - C) \times (D - \text{Index Total Return}) /100]$. Negative numbers in either column mean that the manager underperformed the index for the same reasons. Column G,

"Total," a simple sum of E and F, combines the two factors for that particular industry.

Look to the bottom row of the large box for a quick assessment. Manager C underperformed the index in this quarter. These calculations attribute the poor performance to stock selection (item E, –1.5) more than to industry weighting (item F, –0.9). The table analyzes only one quarter. You need consistent data across a few quarters to draw any conclusions.

Style Analysis

You can also analyze the style of each of your actively managed portfolios. As previously noted, a database can be separated into style universes for an appropriate comparison. In addition to the returns-based style universes in Exhibit 11–5, you could also apply a style definition to each individual security and then categorize a portfolio by the style of securities it holds. For example, you can compare a portfolio comprised of mostly small-cap growth stocks to a universe comprised of small-cap growth portfolios. Exhibit 11–7 shows that ranking. Manager A ranks 43rd in the small-growth equity category.

An important benefit of securities-based style analysis is the ability to easily identify "style drift": A shift in a manager's style. Given the strong historical correlation of style to both return and risk, you can look to style drift analysis to more fully understand what contributes to a manager's return and risk level. In addition, a change in a manager's style will alter any style-driven asset allocation assumptions and potentially undermine your fund's asset allocation strategy. If a manager retained to invest within a certain style drifts away from that style, you will want to address the change.

If your manager was not hired to implement any particular style, style drift may be all right. In fact, it may be part of that manager's investment strategy. Given that value and

EXHIBIT 11–7

Equity Manager Spectrum Style Analysis - Total Returns
Quarter Ending 6/96

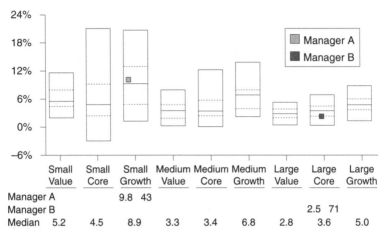

	Small Value	Small Core	Small Growth	Medium Value	Medium Core	Medium Growth	Large Value	Large Core	Large Growth
Manager A			9.8	43					
Manager B							2.5	71	
Median	5.2	4.5	8.9	3.3	3.4	6.8	2.8	3.6	5.0

Source: Canterbury Consulting Services.

growth styles are generally in favor at different times, a manager can maintain high-performance numbers by accurately timing style shifts. However, you will probably avoid this type of manager, since his or her strategy is better suited to individuals with single-manager accounts than foundations and endowment funds that retain multiple managers.

Exhibit 11–8 shows the style movement of managed portfolios and indices through nine possible combinations of both value/growth and capitalization definitions. The vertical axis divides the graph into three capitalization segments: large, mid, and small. The horizontal axis divides the graph by three again to create value, neutral, and growth segments. Once plotted, you can see the style both managers and indices exhibit over a two-year period. The position of an icon within the graph represents the current style definition. Each icon leaves a trail: the lines that emerge from the icon trace the style movement of the manager or index over the past two years.

E X H I B I T   11–8

Equity Manager Spectrum Style Analysis
As of 6/96 (Movement over Past Two Years)

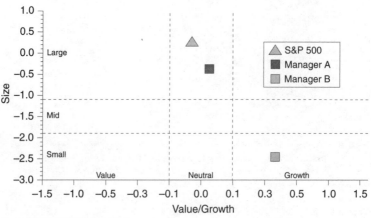

Source: Canterbury Consulting Services.

Although the graph reveals some movement in Manager A's style, this Manager has held to the small-growth category for the past two years. Manager B, while in the large-core (or neutral) category currently, has drifted into both value and growth definitions during the past two years. If this style drift is a violation of your manager guidelines, it is grounds for termination.

Risk Analysis

You must also address the issue of risk and its relationship to return. Too often, an investment committee will focus on returns in the manager selection process, only to discover the risk element later. It is important to track the level of risk the manager assumes in the pursuit of return.

From the risk measurement of individual securities, you can calculate the risk of your portfolio as a whole. Graphs generated from the input and summation of security-level

data offer a fair and easy visual aid for understanding a portfolio's risk level. The structure of these graphs is determined
by the method you choose to measure risk. A variety of
methods for risk measurement exist. It is important that the
measurement you employ accurately reflects your investment committee's conception of risk. Most risk-measure-
ment methods loosely define risk as either potential loss
(downward price movement) or volatility (price fluctuation).
If you prefer to look at risk as the chance for loss, a downside
measure will be most appropriate. If you are comfortable
with volatility as an indicator of risk, you can use beta or
standard deviation.

Beta measures the price volatility of a single security in
relation to the volatility of the entire stock market. By definition the market beta is 1. For example, if the average price
increase in the market is 10 percent, the price of a stock with
a beta of 2 should increase 20 percent (10 percent × 2). The
beta for a portfolio equals the weighted average of the betas
of the individual securities comprising the portfolio.

Standard deviation is probably the most commonly
used method of risk measurement. This method uses the
past performance of securities to determine the range and
probability of possible future performances. The resulting
statistic represents the amount by which future returns are
likely to diverge from expected returns. For example, if
your manager's average return is 10 percent with a standard deviation of 15 percent, it tells you that two-thirds of
the time, short-term returns varied from –5 percent to +25
percent. Statistically, 90 percent of the returns will be within two standard deviations of the mean, or a range of –20
percent to +40 percent.

A related risk measure, the Sharpe Ratio, calculates the
trade-off between reward and volatility. You divide the
portfolio's excess return (return above the risk-free return)
by the portfolio's standard deviation. The higher the Sharpe
Ratio, the more return per unit of risk. The Sortino Ratio is

analogous to the Sharpe ratio except that it measures downside risk, the potential loss with respect to a specified target
return. The potential problem with this—or any downside
measure—is that viable evidence may not exist. If a security's price history doesn't encompass a bear market, you
may have nothing to measure. Statisticians claim that standard deviation gives you a clue as to what the downside
may look like when bad markets return.

Exhibit 11–9 employs standard deviation as the risk
measure. The parameters of the graph are determined by the

EXHIBIT 11–9

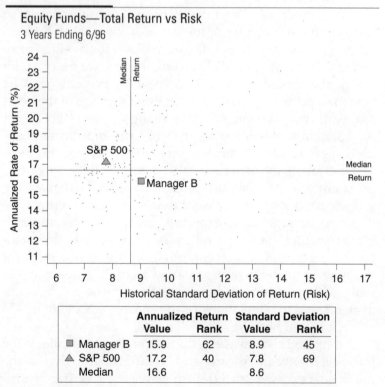

Equity Funds—Total Return vs Risk
3 Years Ending 6/96

	Annualized Return		Standard Deviation	
	Value	Rank	Value	Rank
▢ Manager B	15.9	62	8.9	45
▲ S&P 500	17.2	40	7.8	69
Median	16.6		8.6	

Source: Canterbury Consulting Services.

appropriate universe. The vertical axis represents the range of rates of return. The horizontal axis represents the range of standard deviations. The cross-hairs represent the median risk and return of this universe. Dots plotted on the graph illustrate the dispersion of returns and standard deviations in the universe. The graph shows the three-year average of risk and return.

You can quickly grasp where your fund ranks. In this example, an annualized return of 15.9 percent and a standard deviation of 8.9 puts manager B in the lower right-hand quadrant. This quadrant is the least desirable of the four; the manager assumes greater than average risk to achieve below average return. Ideally you want to be in the upper left quadrant, the so-called northwest quadrant.

No portfolio is risk free. You must weigh the trade-off: In order to limit risk you need to lower your return expectations; to achieve a higher rate of return you must tolerate more risk. The key questions are: Does your manager incur an unnecessary amount of risk to achieve the desired return? Could the same return be realized with less risk?

THE NORMAL PORTFOLIO

When confronted with underperformance relative to an index, a manager will often say something like, "I'm a large-cap manager but I only buy companies with a dividend above the market average and debt below 10 percent of capitalization. *Therefore this index is not really a good benchmark for me."* Consultants have developed the concept of the normal portfolio to address the imperfect fit of a standardized index to a particular manager.

To construct a normal portfolio, one selects securities which fit with a particular manager's "buy criteria." In other words, the normal portfolio for the manager in the example above might include all companies with a market capitalization above $5 billion, dividend yields above that of the S&P 500, and a debt ratio below 10 percent. You could then calculate the return for each of the stocks and the whole "portfolio" over the past quarter. By comparing the manager's return to the returns for the normal portfolio (the stocks he or she could have bought), you gain a sense of the shrewdness of the stock selection. The drawback is that there is no ranking system: you either beat the normal portfolio or you don't.

PORTFOLIO OPPORTUNITY DISTRIBUTION SETS (PODS)

The PODS universe is an advancement of the normal portfolio concept. Developed by Ronald J. Surz, Portfolio Opportunity Distribution Sets provide a framework against which to rank your manager. Unlike a universe of similar (but not exactly comparable) managers a PODS universe has no survivor bias.

One of the problems that makes it difficult to accurately evaluate your fund's performance is that, over time, advisors with poor relative performance tend to lose clients. Eventually the manager may go out of business or merge with a more successful manager or fund. This has the effect of an upward bias on universes. In other words, if your manager ranked right at the 50th percentile over a long period, in reality he or she was in the top half compared to all the managers in the universe at the beginning of the evaluation period. You might say, "So what?" However, if you were forced to erroneously fire an investment advisor by this flawed ranking system, you would have increased the expenses of the fund. (It can cost approximately 2 percent to liquidate one manager's holdings and replace them with those of the successor manager.) Manager "churn" also increases the likelihood that you move to another manager who is an even worse fit for your fund.

To construct a PODS universe, you start with the manager's normal portfolio and then apply the manager's methodology of portfolio construction. For example, she may say, " I use between 35 and 50 stocks, equally weighted. I allow no one security to represent more than 5 percent of the portfolio and no industry to be more than 15 percent of the portfolio." Applying those rules, your computer generates hundreds of random portfolios. You calculate the return for each of the "portfolios" and rank those returns into quartiles. You can then easily compare your manager's results to the universe of returns she could have achieved. Particularly for a more esoteric manager, this may be more accurate than the typical universe or sub-universe comparison.

FIRING MANAGERS

The outcome of the various evaluation procedures we have described is that you may one day be faced with the unhappy task of terminating a manager. At that time you will be especially grateful for having planned ahead. We generally encounter two types of investors: those who rely upon rigid guidelines and those who prefer to weigh each situation. In either case, your investment committee should formulate its policy on this issue **prior** to investing.

Perhaps the most common reason to eliminate a manager is bad performance. However, it's difficult to decide how long to retain a poorly performing manager. A performance evaluation method that uses benchmarks can serve as a convenient, reliable guide. We often recommend the termination of a manager whose performance significantly lags his target market index and his peer group over a three-year period without satisfactory explanation. You may find this criteria too general. Some boards set up a cumulative, step-by-step course of action. For example, underperforming both benchmarks for one quarter puts the

manager "on watch"; four quarters puts him "on proba-
tion"; two years requires that he be fired. In either case, you
should make every effort to understand why a manager
performs poorly. This is the moment when style-based
analysis and performance attribution are invaluable. With
this detailed information, committees can often avoid the
reactive decision to fire a manager "at the bottom."

There are a few nonperformance-related circumstances
that may warrant manager termination. You can think of
them as changes in the structure of the management company that mean you no longer have what you hired.

- A key decision maker on the portfolio management
  team leaves.

- Rapid growth or decrease in accounts occurs,
  threatening the stability of the firm.

- The manager implements a significant change in
  investment methodology.

- The manager exhibits style drift.

- The manager deviates from your policy guidelines.

- The manger loses the passion for the business.

As you can tell from these guidelines, your decision to
fire may be somewhat subjective. If a member of your
board or investment committee loses confidence in a manager for any reason, that may be enough to warrant making
a change.

In the next chapter, we will discuss many of the legal
issues which you face as a fiduciary of an endowment or
foundation. We will cover the third restatement of trusts
which has been adopted by many states.

12
CHAPTER

Fiduciary Issues

OVERVIEW

Trust law has evolved from the time when government securities were considered to be the only prudent investment and trustees were required to make each and every investment decision themselves. Today, fiduciaries face a more flexible and open-ended standard in which reasonable discretion is the limit and the use of professional investment assistance is acceptable. Thus, although today's trustee is required to shoulder the responsibility for difficult but appropriate financial decisions, he or she also has the ability to seek out and use competent professional advisors in fulfilling this responsibility.

HISTORY

The law of trusts dates back centuries to the common law of England. The trust relationship is defined by its parties and their legal relationship to each other. Virtually all trust relationships involve giving to one or more persons, commonly but not always called "trustees," the power to control property in order to provide a benefit not to themselves, but to another. As one might expect in this situation, a fair amount of statutory and case law has developed to govern those empowered to exercise dominion over what is in fact, if not in law, "other people's money."

The familiar trust standard of "the prudent man" is actually a relative latecomer on this scene. That standard was first articulated in a famous 1830 decision of the Massachusetts Supreme Court in the case of *Harvard College v. Amory.*[1] The issue before the court in that case was the nature of a trustee's duty with regard to investment of trust assets. Capsulized, the ruling of the court was that a trustee must exercise the same sound discretion in the management and disposition of trust funds that he or she would use in the management of his or her own affairs.[2]

Despite the flexibility of the prudent man standard, it did not immediately gain universal acceptance. Although many trustees doubtless were pleased by the license given them to make appropriate decisions, they were nonetheless concerned about the fact that their decisions might be "second guessed" by persons with different views. For example, in the 1869 case of *King v. Talbot,*[3] the New York Court of Appeals, the highest court of that state, flatly declared that common stock investments *always* were imprudent trust investments, regardless of the circumstances. Thus, there arose a competing desire for what today would be called a "safe harbor," a method of identifying *in advance*

---

1. 26 Mass. (9 Pic.) 446.
2. The court held that trustees should "observe how men of prudence, discretion and intelligence manage their own affairs, not in regard to speculation, but in regard to the permanent disposition of their funds, considering the probable income, as well as the probable safety of the capital to be invested." 26 Mass. (9 Pic.) at 461.
3. 40 N.Y. 76 (1869).

investments so prudent and appropriate that no one could question the prudence of a trustee who employed them in discharging his or her fiduciary duty.

The demand for certainty prevailed to a large extent in the second half of the nineteenth century. The legislatures of state after state adopted what have become known as "legal lists"—statutory enactments specifying permissible investments for trustees. By 1900, trustees in a majority of states, governing the great majority of the trust funds which then existed, were subject to these statutes.[4]

Because the trust relationship by its very nature involves the management of other people's money, in creating legal lists the various state legislatures were primarily concerned that trustees avoid the loss of trust capital. Thus, it is no surprise that the legal lists of most states were composed of fixed income securities. Equity investments were generally forbidden as being far too speculative and risky.

The safety of fixed income investments was put in question by the Great Depression, which began in 1929. Bond values collapsed. It became apparent that "safe" investments were not always safe. At this point, the "prudent man standard"—by that time more than 100 years old—began to regain favor in the trust community. Today, in one form or another, it is the most common standard against which fiduciary performance is measured.

A second legal rule which evolved in the law of trusts governed *who* was permitted to make a trust's investment decisions. As a rule, the grantor of a trust (the person who first puts assets into a trust) thinks long and hard before selecting the person who will be entrusted with the responsibility of fulfilling the trust's objectives. Historically, the courts tried to effectuate the grantor's decision by insisting

---

4. Shattuck, "The Development of the Prudent Man Rule for Fiduciary Investment in the United States in the Twentieth Century," 12 Ohio State L.J. 491, 499 (1951).

that the designated trustee be the actual decision maker for the trust. Although this rule may have been a workable one where investments were limited to legal lists containing primarily government securities, the rule generated increasing risk to both trusts and their trustees as the financial marketplace became more complex. Today, this rule has largely been replaced with one that permits the use of outside advisors, so long as they are carefully selected and supervised.

THE CURRENT STANDARD(S) GOVERNING FIDUCIARY INVESTMENT PRACTICES

Today, as always, the fiduciary standard applicable to the trustees of endowments and foundations is in a state of flux. Just as there was competition in the nineteenth century between the prudent man standard and legal lists, there exists today a degree of competition among several differing formulations of the prudent man standard. Additionally, there exist several competing formulations of the rule permitting fiduciaries to seek out and use professional investment advisors in making their decisions. The principal standards applied today are discussed below.

IRC Section 4944

Section 4944 of the Internal Revenue Code is one in a series of Code provisions governing private foundations adopted in 1969. It imposes a graduated series of excise taxes on both the foundations and their managers if the foundation "invests any amount in such a manner as to jeopardize the carrying out of any of its exempt purposes."[5] The severity of the penalty depends on how long the foundation continues to hold the "jeopardizing" investment after receiving notice of its jeopardizing status from the Internal Revenue Service.

---

5. I.R.C. § 4944(a)(1).

Initially, the government's approach to the issue addressed by Section 4944 was to call for adoption of what might best be called "reverse" legal lists. A Treasury Department report which preceded enactment of Section 4944 by only four years had called for a law specifically banning investment devices "deemed inherently speculative—as, for example, the purchase of 'puts,' 'calls,' 'straddles,' 'spreads,' 'strips,' 'straps,' and 'special options,' selling short and trading in commodities futures."[6] And the Senate Report that accompanied adoption of Section 4944 had echoed this view, condemning the use of "warrants, commodity futures, and options" and purchases on margin.[7] Ultimately, however, the IRS took a more moderate view. Its regulation interpreting Section 4944 states that an investment will jeopardize a foundation's purpose if the foundation's managers:

> . . . have failed to exercise ordinary business care and prudence, under the facts and circumstances prevailing at the time of making the investment, in providing for the long- and short-term financial needs of the foundation to carry out its exempt purposes . . . [This determination] shall be made on an investment-by-investment basis, in each case taking into account the foundation's portfolio as a whole.[8]

Thus, no specific types of investment have been banned under this provision of the federal law.

The UMIFA

In 1972, the National Conference of Commissioners on Uniform State Laws issued a proposed Uniform Management of Institutional Funds Act. That proposal, intended to govern

---

6. House Comm. on Ways and Means, 89th Cong., 1st Sess., *Treasury Dept. Report on Private Foundations*, 76–717 (Comm. Print 1965) at 45–50.
7. S. Rep. No. 91–552, 91st Cong., 1st Sess. 6, 45 (1969).
8. I.R. Reg. § 53.4944–1(a)(2)(I).

the investment activities of any "incorporated or unincorpo-
rated organization organized and operated exclusively for
educational, religious, charitable, or other eleemosynary purposes, or a governmental organization to the extent it holds
funds exclusively for any of these purposes," does not itself
have the force of law. However, the Commissioners' proposals are influential in the legislatures of many states, and when
officially adopted by a state through legislative action, they
do become the law of the adopting state. In the quarter century that has followed issuance of the Commissioners' proposal, 28 states have adopted it.

Under the UMIFA, the persons responsible for managing a foundation or endowment are required to "exercise
ordinary business care and prudence under the facts and
circumstances prevailing at the time of the action or decision."[9] This was an intentional step away from the historical standard of trust law.[10] "Ordinary business care and
prudence" is the standard applied to the directors of business corporations. Under this standard, directors are
required to behave strictly in good faith, but the level of
prudence demanded is far less rigorous than that historically applied to trustees.

Similarly, that proposed act specifically repudiated the
rule prohibiting trustees from delegating to others their
power to make trust investment decisions. Section 5 of the
UMIFA states:

> [T]he governing Board may (1) delegate to its committees,
> officers or employees of the institution or the fund, or agents,
> including investment counsel, the authority to act in place of
> the board in investment or reinvestment of institutional

---

9. Uniform Management of Institutional Funds Act ("UMIFA"), Section 6 (1972).
10. The author's comment to this provision states: "The [UMIFA] standard is
    generally comparable to that of a director of a business corporation rather
    than that of a private trustee . . ."

funds, (2) contract with independent investment advisors, investment counsel or managers, banks or trust companies, so to act, and (3) authorize the payment of compensation for investment advisory or management services.

Although, one suspects, this provision of the uniform act simply recognized officially the practice that had existed for years, it nonetheless opened the "legal" door to the use of investment professionals in the asset management programs of endowments and trusts.

ERISA

In 1974, Congress enacted a federal law commonly known as ERISA[11] to (among other things) govern the actions of persons serving as fiduciaries of employee benefit plans such as pension funds. Although that statute appeared to embrace the prudent man standard, it did so with a difference. The standard established in that statute was that a "prudent man *acting in a like capacity* and *familiar with such matters* would use in the conduct of an enterprise of like character and with like aims."[12] It thus imported into the prudent man standard elements of expertise, and the flavor of that special relationship that must exist between a trustee and a beneficiary. As often occurs, this federal standard has been "borrowed" by numerous states and enacted into their statutes, in preference to earlier formulations of the prudent man standard.

ERISA is quite explicit about the ability of trustees to make effective use of professional investment advisors. It authorizes fiduciaries to delegate to others their power to invest trust assets in appropriate cases, and it even permits

---

11. The full name of this law is the Employee Retirement Income Security Act of 1974. Its official citation is 29 U.S.C. Section 1001 *et seq.*
12. ERISA Section 404(a)(1)(B).

trust investment *responsibility* to be *transferred* to professional investment advisors under certain circumstances.[13] At
least one court has interpreted ERISA's prudence rule to
require trustees to obtain competent professional investment advice when they are themselves unfamiliar with the
types of investment under consideration.[14]

The UPIA

In 1994, the National Conference of Commissioners on
Uniform State Laws put forward a second proposal of rele-
vance here. Named the Uniform Prudent Investor Act, that
proposal is aimed primarily at the private gratuitous trust.
However, as its authors note, it "also bears on charitable and
pension trusts, among others."[15] The fiduciary standard it
establishes is one of "reasonable care, skill and caution."[16]

Perhaps more than any other of the "models" upon
which the current law of fiduciary responsibility is based,
the UPIA is tied directly to "modern portfolio theory." It
expressly commands that a fiduciary's investment decisions be evaluated "not in isolation but in the context of the
trust portfolio as a whole and as part of an overall investment strategy having risk and return objectives reasonably
suited to the trust."[17]

It adopts the rule that the trustee should ameliorate the
risk of investing by diversifying the fund's assets unless the
purposes of the trust are better served by not diversifying,[18]
and it expressly permits a trustee to delegate investment

---

13. ERISA Section 405(d).
14. *Kataros v. Cody*, 568 F. Supp. 360 (E.D.N.Y. 1983), *affd.* 744 F.2d 270 (2d Cir.,
    1984).
15. Uniform Prudent Investor Act ("UPIA"), Prefatory Note, p. 3 (1994).
16. UPIA, Section 2(a).
17. UPIA, Section 2(b).
18. UPIA, Section 3.

and management functions to others so long as the trustee exercises reasonable care, skill, and caution in selecting the agent, establishing the scope and terms of the delegation, and in periodically reviewing the agent's performance and compliance with the terms of his or her delegation.[19]

POLICING TRUSTEE PERFORMANCE

Candidly, to date, there has been little real judicial enforcement of fiduciary standards against the fiduciaries of endowments and foundations. This may well be due to a longstanding legal concept called "standing," which is intended to define just who can go to court to complain about an action.

In a typical family trust, there is a beneficiary or remainderman who wants to make sure that he or she gets what was promised to them. If they don't get it, they can and do go to court. In the pension arena there are thousands of specifically identifiable persons with enforceable claims against a trust's assets. If they don't receive their pension, they can and do go to court. But who is really in a position to complain when the fiduciaries of an endowment or foundation fall down on the job?

As a rule there also is a specific beneficiary in the case of an endowment. Often, however, that beneficiary has little or no interest in taking a breach of fiduciary duty to court. In some cases, perhaps most, the beneficiary is not an individual but an institution which either itself is the responsible fiduciary or which selected and/or controlled the investment decision maker whose work performance is in question.

In the field of charitable foundations there is seldom any identifiable individual who can say: "I have a *right* to a

---

19. UPIA, Section 9.

distribution, and therefore I have been damaged by the poor investment decision making of the foundation trustees."

In short, in the case of endowments and foundations, usually there is no individual with both the interest and the "standing" to seek judicial relief. Endowments and foundations, however, are not entirely unregulated. In most states the state attorney general has the authority to police them, and of course, where there is money, the Internal Revenue Service is never far away. But in reality considering the substantial portion of our nation's financial resources controlled by endowments and foundations, there has been remarkably little oversight litigation in this area.

Whether this condition will persist far into the future is simply a matter of conjecture. Currently there seems to be a consensus developing that the private sector—in particular, the charitable portion of the private sector—will in the future have to shoulder a greater share of society's burdens. Whether that is "good" or "bad" is beside the point. The point is simply that if this shift does occur, society will begin to pay greater attention to how the assets which provide the services it needs are managed. Therefore, the actions of endowment and foundation trustees will be likely to come under greater scrutiny in the future than they have in the past.

PUTTING IT ALL TOGETHER

Because there are competing formulas for fiduciary prudence—and at least 50 separate jurisdictions, each with its own view of the proper weight to be given to the numerous policy considerations underlying each of these formulations—the only conclusion that can be reached here with certainty is that there is no single rule that will govern everyone. However, it is possible to see with some clarity the direction in which the law of fiduciary investing is moving. Therefore, in the concluding paragraphs of this chapter we will discuss the components of the current view, leaving it to the individual reader to discern when the law which applies in his or her particular jurisdiction will arrive at that point.[20]

First, it seems clear that the "legal list" is dead or dying. In issuing its proposed Uniform Prudent Investment Act in 1994, the National Conference of Commissioners on Uniform State Laws opined:

> Traditional trust law was encumbered with a variety of categoric exclusions. . . . [However,] the universe of investment products changes incessantly. Investments that were at one time thought too risky, such as equities, or more recently, futures, are now used in fiduciary portfolios. By contrast, the investment that was at one time thought ideal for trusts, the long-term bond, has been discovered to import a level of risk and volatility—in this case, inflation risk—that had not been anticipated. . . . The premise [of this proposed law] is that trust beneficiaries are better protected by the Act's emphasis on close attention to risk/return objectives . . . than in attempts to identify categories of investment that are per se prudent or imprudent.[21]

Second, it is now clear that the managers of endowments and foundations have the ability to seek professional investment assistance. The precise conditions that should be documented in order to make certain the decision to seek and use that advice is appropriate for a specific endowment or foundation may vary depending upon the law of the controlling state, but if the persons who are responsible for management of the entity's assets reasonably feel that professional assistance is needed or helpful, that goal should be obtainable. In today's complex and ever-changing financial

---

20. It was not until *1996* that the citizens of Indiana voted to change a state constitutional provision that prohibited the retirement funds of state employees from being invested in equity instruments. Voters had rejected similar proposals twice before in recent years. See T. Eckert, "Bell Rings On Stock Investing," *Indianapolis Business Journal,* Vol. 17, No. 34 (Nov. 11–17, 1996).

21. Drafters' comments to the UPIA, Section 2 (1994).

world, a foundation or endowment without this ability will be in a dangerous position, indeed.

Third, the clear legal trend is to follow the major precepts of *Modern Portfolio Theory*. Among other things, this theory views an investment portfolio not as a collection of individual investments, each of which must meet a fixed standard, but as a unified whole containing numerous components which together must satisfy the applicable standard. While in the past trustees were forbidden or discouraged from investing in anything that might be viewed as a risky investment, the prevailing view among investment professionals is that some risky investments may provide an acceptable means of improving a fund's overall rate of return, so long as the responsible fiduciary takes appropriate action (through other investments) to minimize the risk of loss to the trust.

CONCLUSION

The law of trust investing has always reflected the struggle to balance the need for flexibility on one hand, and the need for certainty on the other, against the obligation of the trustee to fulfill the objectives of his or her trust on both a short- and a long-term basis. The balance has been struck at different points at different times.

Today, the most widely acknowledged standard of fiduciary behavior is that of the "prudent man." Although exactly how prudent that "man" is required to be may vary from state to state, it is clear that in most jurisdictions a trustee is expected to behave more conservatively than the average investor. Most courts, however, are now willing to gauge prudence on a broad basis, thus permitting the fiduciary to take measured risks if, in his or her best judgement, the likely result will be to improve the financial condition of the endowment or foundation for which he or she is responsible.

Although litigation against trustees has been rare, and findings of liability even rarer, there is a real possibility that this condition will change in the future. The increasing importance of endowments and foundations to society in general cannot help but focus increasing public attention on them. Twenty years ago retirement plans fell under similar scrutiny. The expanding volume of fiduciary litigation which today exists against retirement plan fiduciaries under ERISA certainly provides no basis for comfort.

As the complexity of the financial marketplace increases, fewer "nonprofessional" trustees will be able to penetrate that maze without professional guidance of some type. The prudent fiduciary of tomorrow, therefore, is likely to be less an investment technician and more a smart shopper for competent professional assistance and a careful evaluator of professional performance. In this way the financial needs of endowments and foundations can be met without sacrificing the preeminent need for management by someone dedicated to fulfillment of the foundation's or endowment's social goals.

A well thought-out investment policy—one which considers the goals of the trust and the capabilities and informational needs of the fiduciaries as well as the various investment products and services available to satisfy these goals and needs—is certainly the place for a prudent fiduciary to begin the investment process. But that cannot be the end. The financial world changes far too rapidly to permit a fiduciary to rest. Today's fiduciary must also keep his or her eye on the future. Are the investment choices already made achieving their desired result? Have new investment products or methods been developed that are likely to meet the needs of the endowment or foundation with greater certainty or less risk? These, and the many similar questions that will be asked by a prudent fiduciary, demand constant attention and careful oversight of trust assets.

13

CHAPTER

Hiring a Consultant

It's the '90s. By now you've probably come to understand the need for specialization. For the same reasons that you outsource accounting and legal work, you might consider using a consultant to help manage your fund.

If you think that only very large endowments or foundations should use a consultant, think again. Small and mid-sized organizations have less staff, who are probably asked to do more work. Trustees, while often bright, capable people, are volunteers with only so much time to give. A consultant can actually add the most value for smaller funds.

If you're already wearing too many hats and don't have the expertise or staff, if you're concerned about your role as a fiduciary, or if you want to control costs and make your life easier, you may choose to use a consultant.

What do we mean by "consultant"? What can and can't they do for you? How can you find a good one?

Let's start by defining the term. A consultant is an
expert in the design, implementation, and oversight of
investment strategies for endowments and foundations. He
or she is willing, for a fee, to help you improve all areas of
fund management. While banks, insurance companies, and
investment management firms are all willing to give you
advice, we would define a true consultant as an objective,
independent, third party.

Exhibit 13–1 is a questionnaire which can help you
decide if it makes sense for you to use an outside expert. Exhibit 13–2 lists resources to help you locate a consulting firm.

While properly overseeing the management of your
fund may not be rocket science, it is time consuming. And
the stakes—the long-term existence of your fund—are high.

"Time is the currency of the '90s."

EXHIBIT 13–1

Do We Need a Consultant?

Do I have the expertise to handle this project?	yes	no
Do I understand all the fiduciary requirements?	yes	no
Am I clear on all the players and their exact duties (e.g., custodian, trustees, asset manager, etc.)?	yes	no
Can I establish successful spending and investment policies?	yes	no
Do I understand portfolio theory and asset allocation?	yes	no
Do I have the expertise to analyze investment managers or funds?	yes	no
Do I adequately understand risk as well as return?	yes	no
Do I understand the operational/administrative procedures?	yes	no
Do I have enough time to devote to this project?	yes	no
Do I have staff to work on this?	yes	no
Do I have the budget for this (data sources, software, etc.)?	yes	no
Do I even want to do this on my own?	yes	no
Key: Two or more "no" answers—find a consultant!		

Source: DiMeo Schneider & Associates, L.L.C.

Locating a Consultant

Periodicals

Pensions and Investments
965 Jefferson Street
Detroit, MI 48207-3185
Subscriptions:
Jamie Gilmore, 800-678-9595

Pension World Magazine
6151 Powers Ferry Road, Suite 200
Atlanta, GA 30339
Subscriptions:
Carolyn Wright, 404-955-2500

Directories

See *Pensions and Investments*
  above.

Consultant Compendium II
Money Market Directories, Inc.
Box 1608
Charlottesville, VA 22902
800-446-2810

Nelson's Directory of Pension
  Fund Consultants
1 Gateway Plaza
Port Chester, NY 10573
800-333-6357
914-937-8400

Associations

Investment Management
  Consultants Association (IMCA)
9101 E. Kenyon Avenue
Suite 3000
Denver, CO 80237
303-770-3377

The Institute for Investment
  Management Consultants
Box 6123
Scottsdale, AZ 85261-6123
602-922-0090

Source: DiMeo Schneider & Associates, L.L.C.

An experienced consultant has already dealt with every
challenge you'll face. And there's no substitute for objective
advice. Even if you are an expert and have the time to devote
to this task, you still may not have all the resources you need.
Good consulting firms have all the necessary hardware, software, and, most importantly, the people.

PLAYERS VERSUS PRETENDERS

Let's assume that you've made the decision to seek outside
help. You've probably noticed that every salesperson with a
financial product to push now calls himself or herself a consultant. How can you identify the real thing?

It's relatively easy. A true consultant makes virtually all of his or her revenue from consulting; it is not a part-time occupation. A good consultant should *never* recommend his or her firm's money management or financial products. And he or she should be able to provide you with numerous references from current clients. IMCA's Code of Professional Responsibility (Exhibit 13–3) will give you a good sense of the proper mindset.

EXHIBIT 13–3

Investment Management Consultants Association Code of Professional Responsibility

Each professional investment management consultant shall:

- Serve the financial interests of clients. All recommendations to clients and decisions on behalf of clients shall be solely in the interest of the clients.
- Disclose fully to clients services provided and compensation received. All financial relationships, direct or indirect, between consultants and investment managers, plan officials, beneficiaries, sponsors, or others shall be fully disclosed.
- Provide to clients all requested information as well as other information they may need to make informed decisions. All client inquiries shall be answered promptly, completely, and truthfully.
- Maintain the confidentiality of all information entrusted by the client, to the fullest extent permitted by law.
- Comply fully with all statutory and regulatory requirements affecting the delivery of consulting services to clients.
- Endeavor to establish and maintain excellence in all aspects of investment management consulting (or all aspects of financial services to clients).
- Support and participate in the activities of the Investment Management Consultants Association to enhance the investment management consulting profession.
- Maintain the highest standard of personal conduct.

Source: Investment Management Consultants Association (IMCA)
                9101 E. Kenyon Avenue, Suite 3000
                Denver, Colorado 80237
                303/770-3377.

Exhibit 13–4 is a sample Request for Proposal (RFP) which you can adapt for your own use. As with all RFPs, shorter is better. Ask only for information that will help you make a decision. Identify only those services you need.

EXHIBIT 13–4

RFP for Consulting Services

I. Background
   A. The Firm:
      Name: _____
      Location: _____
      Size (revenues): _____ Employees: _____
   B. Person Responding:
      Name: _____
      Title: _____
      What percentage of your income comes from consulting activities?
      _____
      Identify other sources of income: _____
      _____
   C. Organization:
      Describe the structure of your firm's consulting group: _____
      _____
      _____
      _____
   D. Experience:
      Number of not-for-profit clients: _____
      How many clients have you added in the past two years? _____
      How many clients have you lost? _____
      Why? _____
      _____
      _____

II. Expertise
   A. Technology:
      Describe hardware and software which will be used on our project:

Exhibit 13–4, *continued*

_____

_____
_____
_____

Describe your database of investment managers: _____
_____
_____
_____

Describe your due diligence efforts regarding those managers:_____
_____
_____
_____

B. Personnel:
   Who will be our primary contact? _____
   Backup contact person: _____
   How many clients does each consultant advise? _____
   Who performs the following functions?
        Manager search: _____
        Performance evaluations: _____
        Asset allocation studies: _____
        Investment policies: _____
   Please attach a brief biography of each of the people mentioned above.
C. What sets you apart as a firm? _____
   _____
   _____
   _____

D. Provide three references of clients similar to our organization:
   1. Name: _____ Title: _____
      Organization: _____
      Phone: _____
   2. Name: _____ Title:_____
      Organization: _____
      Phone: _____

Exhibit 13–4, *concluded*

    3. Name: _____ Title: _____
    Organization: _____
    Phone: _____

III. The Project

    Based on your understanding of our needs, please attach your responses to the following:

    A. Describe the services which you propose.

    B. Who will provide each of these services?

    C. Describe any additional capabilities.

    D. Please attach samples of the following:

        Asset allocation report

        Manager search project

        Performance evaluation report

IV. Fees

    A. Quote fees for each service provided.

       Do you also work on a retainer basis? (Please quote.)

    B. Describe your policy on soft dollars.

Source: DiMeo Schneider & Associates, L.L.C.

PRACTICAL HINTS

- Send your RFP only to viable candidates. For example, if you know in advance that you would not really consider the consulting department of a large broker-dealer, don't waste your time and theirs.
- Try to narrow the list of candidates before you send out the questionnaire.
- Keep the RFP short and insist on complete, but concise responses.
- Describe your minimum selection requirements. This will keep non-candidates from wasting your time and theirs.

When you call the references, Exhibit 13–5 may prove useful. These are some effective questions to help solicit information that the reference might not volunteer.

EXHIBIT 13–5

Consultant Reference Questionnaire

1. How long have you worked with _____ [the consulting firm]?
2. What do they do best?
3. Where is there room for improvement?
4. Describe how they reduce your workload.
5. What could have been streamlined?
6. Rate their capabilities in each of these areas from highest (5) to lowest (1):

    Goal setting/design

    Spending policies

    Asset allocation

    Manager search

    Performance evaluation

    Pricing

    Overall client service

Note: This is designed for a phone interview. Although the list of questions is short, it is designed to uncover areas of weakness. It's important to keep the questions in this order.

Source: DiMeo Schneider & Associates, L.L.C.

THE PLAYERS

There are three main types of consultants: Large actuarial and benefits consulting firms; separate departments within brokerage firms; and independent consulting firms. Each has strengths and weaknesses (see Exhibit 13–6). Regardless of what each type may say about its competition, you can reasonably expect high levels of service from all three.

HOW TO CHOOSE

If you believe you'll need assistance in other areas (such as benefits or compensation) you might lean toward the large benefits consulting firms. On the other hand, if you need

EXHIBIT 13–6

Consultant Pros and Cons

Large Consulting/Actuarial Firms

Pros
- Expertise and experience
- Impartial
- High-quality standards

Cons
- May be expensive
- May have cursory understanding of investments

Brokerage Firms

Pros
- Huge resources
- Financial expertise
- Cost-competitive

Cons
- There is a big difference between a broker and a consultant (make certain that they maintain an independent consulting group and that you're not talking to a mere salesperson without the expertise you need)
- Potentially biased

Independents

Pros
- Specialized expertise
- Cost-effective
- Can be highly flexible
- Focused and attentive

Cons
- May have limited resources
- May not have financial strength or staying power

Source: DiMeo Schneider & Associates, L.L.C.

specialized expertise or unusual services, you might look at the independents. The consulting efforts of brokerage firms may fall somewhere in between. If you are unsure, look at all three. Be sure that all the firms you consider have significant experience in consulting endowments and foundations.

Once you've sent out the RFPs and evaluated the answers, it is time to narrow the field. Make your life easy; do not bring in more than three finalists.

THE INTERVIEW

You'll already know most of the quantitative information about the finalists before the face-to-face meeting. Presumably all are competent. What, then, do you want to learn in the interview?

First of all, which of the candidates best fits with your objectives? Personal compatibility is important as well. You will be working closely with the consultant on important projects with tight deadlines; don't be too quick to overlook personality quirks which may become hugely irritating when you are in constant contact.

Try to understand the philosophy of the firm. If you share a common point of view, many of the details will fall into place. If you have philosophical differences, odds are you'll end up with friction.

A few years ago we conducted a manager search for a large endowment. Our client has a culture which values top-quality job performance, but an unassuming, down-to-earth demeanor. The trustees had narrowed the list of candidates to three finalists. All the proposals looked good; the references were stellar. One candidate, however, seemed to have a decided edge. This firm offered the lowest cost, and investment performance seemed more than acceptable. In fact, two of the trustees were ready to hire the firm sight unseen. However, at the interview the leading candidate's representatives seemed so smug and arrogant that each trustee voted thumbs down. The Chair of the Investment Committee commented: "There's no way we could hire them. We have a policy here, no jerks!"

There has to be a fit, whether you're choosing a consultant or an investment manager.

Get Proof

In the interview, ask for a demonstration or specific examples. If this is a service that you need, don't let them tell you how good they are—make them prove it. Have each candidate review your fund specifics prior to the meeting and make observations and suggestions. You'll quickly judge for yourself who's good and who's not.

Ask for Verification

What have they done for other clients? How have the strategies they've recommended performed? Get the numbers.

Exhibit 13–7 gives you some sample interview questions. Make sure you ask each finalist the same questions. Keep your list of questions relatively short. You won't get through a long list anyway. Finally, ask open-ended questions ("essay questions"). You want to learn how they think.

EXHIBIT 13–7

Consultant Interview Questions

Why do you want to do business with us?
Describe your ideal client.
What sets you apart?
What is your greatest shortcoming?
How would you foresee helping us?
When you don't win a competition, why do you lose?
How many clients have you lost in the past year?
Why did they leave?
If I were to hire two consulting firms, what would I hire you for?
  What would I hire the other firm to do?
What steps have you taken to eliminate conflict of interest with
  regard to fund or manager selection?

Note: Most factual information should come from the response to the RFP. Of course, any questions that are raised by a response should be addressed.

Source: DiMeo Schneider & Associates, L.L.C.

THE ON-SITE VISIT

Visit your candidates in their shop. Everyone can talk about their capabilities, but it is quite another thing to show you the hardware, software, and personnel who will be working with your organization.

THE CONTRACT

Once you've made your decision, get the agreement in writing. What services are they to provide? What remedies do you have if they don't meet your expectations? What is the term of the contract? How do they bill?

We suggest you request the right to end the contract with 30 days written notice and to be obligated only for services rendered up to that point.

Have your attorney review the contract. We are not in the business of rendering legal advice, so we have intentionally excluded a sample contract or worksheet. Suffice it to say, legal review is not the area in which to cut costs.

FEES

Fees are typically quoted in one of three ways:

1. *Project basis.* There is a fee for each specific service; e.g., X dollars for an investment policy, Y dollars for a manager search, and so on.

2. *Retainer.* An annual fee to include all services. If your needs are fairly broad, the retainer may be more cost-effective. For example, a consulting firm may quote:

   Goal setting and policies $5,000

   Asset allocation $10,000

Manager search (each)	$5,000
Performance monitoring	$8,000
Total	$28,000

However, the retainer fee may be only $20,000.

3. *Asset based.* Sometimes a retainer fee is quoted as a percentage of assets under management rather than a set figure. If you are operating on a tight budget, an asset-based fee can make sense. Depending on the size of the fund and the amount of service provided, asset-based fees might range from 3 basis points for a very large fund to 50 basis points for a small fund. A basis point is 1/100 of 1 percent.

EFFECTIVE USE OF A CONSULTANT

How do you get your money's worth after you've hired a consulting firm? First of all, think of them as an extension of your staff. Help them understand what you want. Also, help them understand your organization, including the personalities of the players.

Secondly, give them as much of the work as possible. They'll let you know if they don't consider a certain task to be a part of their assignment. If you're unsure of which way to go at key turning points, let them research the alternatives. For example, what impact would a 1 percent increase in your spending policy have? Tell the consultant you want a succinct presentation of the pros and cons as they apply to your needs. Let them create the detailed backup.

Ask them to explain their process. How do they come to their conclusions? For instance, if you are conducting an investment manager search, get the details. How are candidates to be screened? You may want to add or subtract certain criteria.

Use their experience. They probably know what works and what doesn't. Trust them. For example, if your committee wants 11 different fund choices, but the consultant says that 5 or 6 will be sufficient and a more manageable number, listen. Obviously, you control the decision, but be open minded.

Finally, if you don't understand something, make the consultant explain. Part of their job is to educate you. Let them make you better trustees.

In the next chapter, we'll discuss reducing costs. Unfortunately, too many trustees ignore this crucial step . . . to the detriment of their funds.

14

CHAPTER

Reduce Costs

All trustees should get a fix on expenses and try to drive costs to a minimum. It is especially important for endowments and foundations. Because expenses eventually are reflected in performance, costs eat into your fund and make your return target that much more difficult to achieve.

This chapter identifies many opportunities for cost reduction. As you can see in Exhibit 14–1, controlling expenses can have a huge impact on your fund.

ELIMINATE THE UNNECESSARY

Certain expenses are simply unjustifiable. In today's competitive environment, it makes no sense to purchase investments with front-end sales charges or any exit/surrender fees. Some mutual funds and insurance contracts impose commissions that take a big bite out of your return. In every

EXHIBIT 14–1

$10,000,000 Endowment Growth in 20 Years*

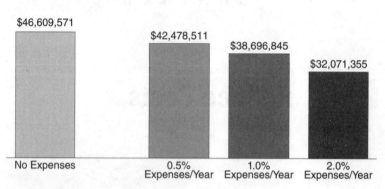

* Assumes 8% Earnings.

Source: DiMeo Schneider & Associates, L.L.C.

imaginable scenario, you can locate equally attractive
investments without such fees.

Furthermore, review your fund for redundant services
and charges. Eliminate them! Endowments and foundations evolve over time and it's not unusual that a fund
receives the same service from two providers (at twice the
necessary cost). For example, perhaps your custodian provides a portfolio analysis showing performance vs. various
indices as well as cost and current value of each position.
However, you've also contracted with a consulting firm to
provide a very detailed performance report. It might make
sense to eliminate the custodian's report (and obtain a
reduction of their fee).

MINIMIZE THE NECESSARY

Many expenses cannot be avoided and, in fact, are justified.
The key is to minimize cost. Remember, you always want
value, whatever the cost.

Investment Management Fees

Once you develop a blueprint, you hire investment managers to implement it within their area of expertise. The managers expect to be paid. A competent manager should add plenty of value over time. However, there is a disturbing trend which costs the average endowment money.

Although investment management fees have fallen in many circumstances, there are exceptions. Mutual funds have enjoyed an exponential growth in the amount of money under management. Though fees should decrease as assets surge, this has not been the case. As Exhibit 14–2 demonstrates, fund fees have actually increased.

The mutual fund industry has a semilogical explanation for this: although assets have grown substantially, the services that funds provide to shareholders have grown at an even faster pace. Toll-free phone numbers and printed educational materials are costly. Funds say that it's a wonder they deliver at as low a price as they do. However, as an institutional investor you should seek out cost advantages that are rightfully yours.

EXHIBIT 14–2

Mutual Fund Expenses
Stock Fund Averages

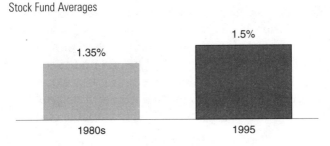

Source: Morningstar, Inc.

Explore these suggestions:

1. *Use separate account management.* In a sense, the
   fund companies are right. Funds provide numerous services to tens of thousands of shareholders,
   most with small account balances. Fortunately, you
   only seek one service from a money manager:
   investment management. Furthermore, you probably have much more to invest than an individual.
       At a certain point, it is more cost effective to
   hire an investment manager who will purchase
   individual securities on your behalf, rather than to
   pool your money with other investors in a mutual
   fund. It's not unusual for separate account management to cut your cost in half. There are other potential benefits. With a separate account, the investment strategy can be tailored to your needs. Also,
   ongoing performance will not be influenced by cash
   inflows or outflows of other investors.

2. *Purchase institutional mutual funds or commingled
   trusts.* Certain funds are available only to institutional investors. Such funds are often managed by the
   same portfolio managers as their retail counterparts
   but generally have higher minimum investment
   requirements and significantly lower expenses.

3. *Seek low-cost retail funds.* Sometimes, for one reason
   or another (perhaps the amount you're investing in a
   certain asset class is small), you have to purchase a
   retail fund. No problem. Just be certain to seek funds
   that meet all your criteria, including low expenses.
   With more than 8,000 mutual funds, you should be
   able to purchase good funds at reasonable costs.

*Special note: Again, when we reference cost, we mean the
internal expense ratio of a mutual fund or the advisory fee of a*

*separate account manager, not front-end charges or surrender charges. **Never** pay a front-end fee!*

Trustee/Custodial Fees

Most endowments and foundations use at least several investment advisors/funds (e.g., a separate account manager, a mutual fund, and a bank commingled trust). While each manages a portion of the fund, the trustee acts as a central custodian for all assets and provides a comprehensive account statement.

Trustee fees can vary significantly. Be sure to find a trustee that does a lot of business with not-for-profit organizations. Some offer services to endowments and foundations at an attractive discount from their standard price structure.

Trading

Review trading costs if you use separate account management. And when you do, pay attention to both commissions and trade execution.

Commissions on stock transactions are fairly easy to determine. They are usually expressed as a cents-per-share rate. Although simple to monitor (and negotiate), many small and mid-size institutions grossly overpay on commissions. If you still operate on a full commission or a 25 percent discount, you're overpaying.

Convert commissions to a flat cents-per-share rate. An appropriate range is 5¢ to 15¢ per share depending on the size of your fund.

It's a bit more difficult to evaluate commissions charged on a bond transaction. The purchase or sale is usually quoted as a *net* price. Ask your investment manager to describe his or her approach to trading bonds. Most get quotes from two or three brokers and push for a competitive price (after all, if they overpay it is reflected in performance).

While commissions are important, trade executions can have a much greater impact on performance. How well does your manager buy that new stock she adds to your portfolio? Does she take it on the chin when she goes to sell a security? Sometimes the commission may be very reasonable, say 8¢ per share, but the execution is lousy. Poor execution on stock transactions can have a "hidden" cost of ⅛ or a ¼ per share (12½¢ or 25¢). This hidden cost comes straight out of performance.

Fortunately, most managers seek good execution because poor execution hurts their performance. And ultimately, they must live or die by their performance. Totally captive arrangements, such as some brokerage wrap accounts, should be carefully analyzed.

Special note: Our comments on trading costs (both commissions and execution) focus only on separate accounts. You have little, if any, control over trading activity with a mutual fund or commingled trust.

Consulting

Consultants can bring a lot to the table. However, some offer more value than others. See Chapter 13 for more detail on the cost-effective use of your consultant.

ADDITIONAL TIPS

1. *Negotiate.* It won't hurt you to ask for a better deal. There's something very compelling about the statement, "The business is yours, if you can lower your fee by . . . ."

2. *Request "most-favored-nation" clauses.* A "most-favored-nation" clause states that no similar client receives a better deal from a given provider. Request this clause even if you oversee a small fund, but be sure to ask how they monitor and ensure compliance with their commitments.

3. *Use commission recapture.* Your fund may "recapture" commissions generated in the normal course of asset management. These recaptured dollars can be used to pay for other services. This approach is increasingly used and perfectly appropriate as long as the commissions fall within the area of "best price and execution."

Here's how commission recapture works. An endowment or foundation directs its money manager to place a percentage of its trades through a specific broker/dealer (at a competitive commission rate). The fund earns a credit of perhaps 50 to 70 percent of the commission paid. The commission recapture broker(s) writes a check to pay for your various expenses. You merely pass on invoices from vendors such as custodians, consultants, and auditors.

It is extremely important to make certain that you obtain good trade execution. If you save 3¢ per share but lose an ⅛ (12.5¢), poor execution can cost your fund thousands of dollars per year. A good consultant can help you evaluate commission recapture programs. If you prefer to do the research on your own, look for the following:

- A high percentage of agency business. An agent effects a transaction between buyer and seller. A principal buys from one client and sells to another (an added layer of cost).
- Large block order flow. This tells you the firm is a player.

- A high percentage of "agency crosses." Buyer and seller meet at a favorable price (often in the middle of the normal bid-asked spread).

If you're still in doubt, ask your managers about the brokerage firm's executions. As a last resort you can commission a study which attempts to measure and rank executions.

Over time, expenses will have a significant impact on your fund's performance. Do your best to eliminate the unnecessary costs and minimize the others.

15 CHAPTER

Conclusion

*T*oday was the day. After months of preparation, they would succeed where all the others had failed. He shaded his eyes against the tropical sunlight as he tried to spot the buoy among the blinding reflections.

Right from the beginning he had treated this as business, not some adventure. His goal was to raise the **Nueve Monos**. She had gone down in 1598. Fifteen tons of plundered gold had made her too heavy to ride out the sudden storm so typical of these waters.

He remembered the hours spent in the musty depths of the maritime library in Cadiz. His trip to Wood's Hole had helped him to understand the effects of four centuries of powerful underwater currents. Monte Carlo simulations on a borrowed Cray computer suggested this area of the ocean floor.

He had tried methodically to stack the deck in their favor. Satellite guidance systems created an invisible grid, and he hired the best divers to execute the search. The undersea imaging equipment *had been developed for deep water oil exploration. Day by day, he monitored their progress. Twenty-two hours ago his radio had crackled with the news: "We've located what appears to be a wreck." They had placed a buoy and awaited the arrival of the vacuum lift dredge. Now all was in place.*

When he first followed the buoy cable to the bottom, he remembered some of the dangers of these waters: The barracuda, the blue shark, and the sawfish, which could cut a man in half with one shake of its razor-edged snout. However, there were only bright schools of damsel fish and wrasse darting in synchronized patterns through the clear water.

Two of the divers were handling the vacuum lift. As they swept the head across the ocean floor, tons of sand and shell were sucked away in a swirling cloud. A blackened timber appeared in the widening pit. A few more minutes of work and the ribs of a hull were obvious. He gripped the mouthpiece in his teeth and felt his breathing grow fast and shallow. Suddenly, he gestured for them to cut the suction. He swam to the base of the pit. As the water cleared, he searched for the metallic glint that he'd seen a moment ago. There! Partially protruding from beneath a blackened rib was a dark crusted shape. Along one side was a gouge caused by the swirling debris, and gleaming through the scratched crust was the warm luster of gold. They had found the Nueve Monos!

In your search for investment success, you must be as well prepared. Take advantage of all the tools and techniques which have been developed in the past few years.

Challenges certainly lie ahead. Hopefully, the information you have gleaned from this book will help you face them. The oversight of foundation and endowment assets has never been easy. Now it promises to become even more difficult. Although suits against trustees and other fiduciaries have been relatively rare to this point, we do live in a litigious society. You are wise to take your responsibilities seriously and to invest with prudence. The steps we suggest should help you do so.

The capital markets themselves have grown more complex as they have become increasingly dominated by large institutions. The professionals who manage these large pools of assets can be quick to buy or sell, and information moves with the speed of a scrolling cursor. Automated trading systems make it possible to buy or sell billions of dollars worth of securities with the push of a button. Traders can receive, analyze, and act on news almost as it unfolds. Furthermore, "market hours" no longer exist; trading activity in U.S. stocks and bonds circles the globe. As a result, market advances and declines are accelerated.

Financial tools and strategies are created in the laboratory of academia and then tested in the real world with hundreds of millions of dollars on the line. Some have been spectacular failures; the collapse of "portfolio insurance" in the stock market crash of 1987 is one example. Academics have taken Modern Portfolio Theory and its offspring in new and sometimes startling directions. The exponential increase in computing power allows the analysis of millions of bits of information . . . the goal? An edge!

In the sort of environment we just described, the old seat-of-the-pants approach to the oversight of your portfolio is no longer a competitive option. You need to follow an effective, step-by-step procedure. To summarize the steps we covered in this book:

1. *Set goals.* Develop a clear understanding of your objectives, spending requirements, and tolerance for risk.

2. *Develop a written investment policy.* Set down in writing your goals and the strategies for implementing them. This will be your game plan. Establish procedures in the clarity of forethought rather than in the chaos of an emergency. A written policy avoids confusion and builds a framework for continuity.

3. *Allocate assets.* Virtually all academic research indicates that asset allocation is the most crucial decision your committee can make. With over 90 percent of your investment results on the line, take advantage of the tools and techniques which are now available. This definitely is not a "guesstimate" step.

4. *Allocate styles.* Research shows that a manager's investment style determines over 90 percent of his or her performance. Again, take advantage of the technology that has been developed in the past few years to avoid inadvertent (and often ill-timed) style bets.

5. *Hire professional managers.* The first four steps create the game plan for your fund. Hire the appropriate stable of money managers and/or mutual funds to implement your game plan. Avoid the "rookie mistakes" we described in Chapters 9 and 10. Although asset allocation and style allocation determine the bulk of your results, money management can ultimately add (or cost you) millions of dollars!

6. *Evaluate performance.* Every enterprise needs to regularly evaluate results. A store that never takes inventory will go broke within a few years! It's not enough to put good managers in place and hope for the best. If your fund was a qualified plan operating under the ERISA laws, you would be *required* to monitor your performance regularly and take action if warranted. It is especially prudent for endowments and foundations to implement a systematic evaluation process, since they are not subject to the same external controls as qualified plans. Besides, it's just common sense.

The principles outlined above have their basis in the most current academic research. However, we have opted to spare you most of the math and statistical studies. Instead, we've attempted to give you a pragmatic approach which is both understandable and actionable. It is our hope that this will help you develop a reasonable strategy for the investment of your fund and the conviction to stick with that strategy.

GOING FORWARD

We strongly suggest that you view the asset management of your fund as an ongoing mission rather than a one-time event. The world turns; capital markets continue to evolve. Portfolio theory is, at best, an imperfect science. Therefore, make it a practice to continually scan the financial horizon for new techniques and information which can help your fund achieve its goals.

In the past few years alone, we have made great strides. Returns-based style analysis was added to the tool kit only in the early 1990s. Downside risk analysis and the work of Frank Sortino are also fairly recent developments. The point is that you need to continually refresh your knowledge base so that you stay up to speed. But don't go it alone. Exhibit 15–1 provides a list of resources which can alert you to new developments.

Once, only the largest funds could afford to avail themselves of expert advice. Now smaller endowments and foundations can also tap those resources. Prudent fund oversight is not an easy, do-it-yourself project. The simple fact is, if you don't follow the steps we've outlined in this book, you are unlikely to achieve the investment success you seek. If you don't have the time and training to thoroughly follow the path, hire an independent third party that does.

EXHIBIT 15–1

Resources

Publications	Institutional Investor
The Journal of Investing 488 Madison Avenue New York, NY 10022 212-224-3185	488 Madison Avenue New York, NY 10022 212-224-3185
Journal of Portfolio Management 488 Madison Avenue New York, NY 10022 212-224-3185	*Pensions and Investments* 965 E. Jefferson Avenue Detroit, MI 48207 800-678-9595
Financial Analysts Journal P.O. Box 3668 Charlottesville, VA 22903 804-980-3668	*Pension World* 35 W. Wacker Drive, Suite 700 Chicago, IL 60601 312-726-7277
CFO Magazine 111 W. 57th Street, 11th Floor New York, NY 10019 212-459-3004	

Source: DiMeo Schneider & Associates, L.L.C.

CLOSING WORDS

We wish you great success. As we said at the outset, those who act as fiduciaries for most endowments and foundations are among the best and the brightest of our society. And smart people make good decisions if they are given the right facts. Hopefully we have given you enough information to point you in the right direction. You serve a noble cause and deserve our best wishes in your efforts.

INDEX

Manager/fund searches (*Cont.*):
  performance evaluation in, 114,
    121, 129–131, 135–162
  pitfalls of, 9–10
  preparing for, 117–118
  proxy voting in, 135
  social investing and, 134–135
  style in, 102–103
    (*See also* Investment style; Style
    analysis)
  tenure in, 114–116, 120
  three-swing approach to, 113–116,
    118–128
  trade execution in, 134
Manager Questionnaire (IMCA),
  135–162
Margin calls, 98
Market capitalization, 86, 90, 110, 115,
  118, 165–166
Market indices, as benchmarks, 32, 84,
  132, 165–171
Market timing, problems of, 9, 62–63
Markowitz, Harry, 7, 50–51
Massachusetts Supreme Court, 188
Maturity, 87–89
McDonald's, 12
Mean/variance analysis, 54–55
Merrill Lynch, 166
Mid-cap companies, 86
Mission statement:
  goals and, 16–17
  in investment policy statement,
    30, 34
Mobius Group, Inc., 102, 130, 171
Modern Portfolio Theory (Markowitz), 7
Modern Portfolio Theory (MPT), 49,
  50–57, 70–71
  correlation coefficient and, 53–54,
    70
  efficient frontier in, 50
  return and, 18, 51, 52, 56–57, 71
  risk and, 50, 51, 52, 54–56, 71
  Uniform Prudent Investor Act
    (UPIA) and, 194–195, 197, 198
Money managers (*see* Portfolio
  managers)

Moody's, Inc., 87
Morgan Stanley Europe, Australia,
  and Far East Index (EAFE), 51, 52
Morningstar, Inc., 111–113, 118, 130
Most-favored-nation clauses, 133, 221
Multifactor models, 89–90, 92, 94
Multiple benchmarks, 166–167
Mutual funds:
  commissions and fees of, 215–216,
    217–219
  index funds, 131–133, 165
  institutional, 218
  portfolio managers versus,
    110–113, 133
  ranking of, 110–113
  returns on, 129–131
  searching for (*see* Manager/fund
    searches)
  separate account management, 218

National Conference of
  Commissioners on Uniform State
  Laws, 191–193, 194, 197
*Nelson's Directory of Investment
  Advisors*, 82–83
*Nelson's Directory of Pension Fund
  Consultants*, 203
New York Court of Appeals, 188–189
Normal portfolio, 183–185
  construction of, 183–184
  Portfolio Opportunity Distribution
    Sets (PODS), 184–185

"Old boy" network, 10
On-site visits, 212
Optimized allocations, 71–73

Pan American Airlines, 20
Passive management, active management versus, 131–133, 167–168
Past performance:
  in determining expected returns,
    56–57, 71–72

ABOUT THE AUTHORS

William A. Schneider, CIMA

Bill is a Managing Director of DiMeo Schneider & Associates, L.L.C., a Chicago based firm that provides advisory services to endowments, foundations and plan sponsors. DiMeo Schneider & Associates is a Registered Investment Adviser under the Investment Advisers Act of 1940.

Bill served as Senior Vice President with Kidder, Peabody's PRIME Asset Consulting Group before co-founding DiMeo Schneider & Associates. He currently advises over 20 qualified plans, including several leading midwest law firms and Fortune 100 companies. He has written and lectured extensively on topics of retirement plan oversight and has co-authored articles for publications such as *Pension World Magazine.* Bill is co-author of the book *Designing a 401(k) Plan.* He holds the title Certified Investment Management Analyst, awarded through the IMCA accreditation program at the Wharton School of Business. Bill graduated from the University of Illinois in 1967 and has completed advanced training in asset allocation and portfolio theory.

Robert A. DiMeo, CIMA, CFP

Bob is a Managing Director of DiMeo Schneider & Associates,
L.L.C., a Chicago-based firm that provides advisory services
to endowments, foundations, and plan sponsors. DiMeo
Schneider & Associates is a Registered Investment Adviser
under the Investment Advisers Act of 1940.

Prior to cofounding DiMeo Schneider & Associates, Bob
served as vice president for Kidder, Peabody's Institutional
Consulting Group, where he chaired the 401(k) Committee.

He has authored and been the subject of numerous arti-
cles appearing in prominent publications, including the *Los
Angeles Times, Crain's Chicago Business,* and *Pension World
Magazine,* and has taught courses on fiduciary responsibili-
ty and related subjects. Bob co-authored *Designing A 401(k)
Plan* (Chicago: Irwin, 1995), has served as reviewing editor
for the *CCH Pension Plan Guide* (Chicago: Commerce
Clearing House, 1995), and is a member of the Ethics
Committee for the Investment Management Consultants'
Association (IMCA).

Bob obtained the title Certified Investment Management
Analyst from IMCA's accreditation program at the Wharton
School of Business, and the Certified Financial Planner
accreditation from the College for Financial Planning. He
obtained his bachelor's degree from Bradley University.

D. Robinson Cluck

"Bob" Cluck, Managing Director, is a founder of Canterbury Consulting, a division of Canterbury Capital Services, which was established in 1988 by four former associates of Kidder, Peabody & Company, Inc., and is now owned by six employee shareholders. Canterbury Consulting is a Registered Investment Adviser under the Investment Advisers Act of 1940 and focuses exclusively on providing investment consulting services.

Canterbury currently provides consulting services to approximately 75 institutional clients whose aggregate assets exceed $2.5 billion. Consulting services are directed by four senior consultants who have provided a full range of investment services to public and private retirement funds, foundations, endowments, and high-net-worth individuals for more than 17 years on average.

Bob was also a founder, principal, and vice president of the Institutional Consulting Services of Kidder, Peabody & Company, Newport Beach, from 1980 until 1988, when he left to form Canterbury Consulting. From 1978 to 1980, he was with Smith Barney Harris Upham & Company. He holds an economics degree from the University of California at Irvine and an MBA from Pepperdine University.

Matthew R. McArthur

In 1992, after practicing for more than twenty years with the Chicago law firm of Pope, Ballard, Shepard and Fowle, Ltd., Matthew R. McArthur established M. R. McArthur & Associates, Ltd., a Hinsdale, Illinois law firm with a national practice specializing in employee relations and benefits. While at Pope, Ballard, Mr. McArthur served as a Director of the firm's Labor and Employment Law Department for fifteen years and, beginning in 1986, as Chairman of its Employee Benefits Department. Mr. McArthur received his BA degree in Economics and Business Administration (with honors) from Knox College in 1964, and in 1967 he received his JD degree (with distinction) from the Duke University School of Law. He has been admitted to the practice of law in Illinois, and before federal courts throughout the country including the Supreme Court of the United States.

In his practice, Mr. McArthur represents primarily small and mid-size employers in matters pertaining to all phases of employment relations and benefits. Mr. McArthur also serves as independent ERISA counsel to plans themselves. He deals regularly with a wide range of benefit related matters such as collective bargaining with respect to employee benefits, the defense of multi-employer plan collection and withdrawal liability assessment cases, and all issues relating to the design and administration of both qualified and non-qualified executive and employee retirement, medical and other benefit plans. Mr. McArthur's practice philosophy emphasizes prudence and compliance with ERISA's fiduciary requirements as the best means of protecting both plan participants and the fiduciaries who serve them. He counsels plan fiduciaries, and assists them with compliance in their complex statutory and regulatory obligations, particularly with regard to benefit administration, reporting and disclosure, claims appeals, contractual relations with independent investment and other service providers, and the monitoring of service provider performance.

Mr. McArthur is a member of the Illinois and American Bar Associations, and he has served on a number of committees of the ABA's Sections on Labor Law and Litigation and its Forum Committee on the Construction Industry. He is co-chairman of the ABA Labor Section's subcommittee on collective bargaining and employee benefits. He is a national board member of both the Investment Management Consultants Association, and of WEB, a nation-wide network of professionals working in employee benefits. He has published numerous articles in the field of employee benefits, and has spoken on benefit related subjects before audiences at the Wharton School and at other locations from coast to coast.